Georg Ossian Sars

An account of the Crustacea of Norway,

With short descriptions and figures of all the species - Vol. 1

Georg Ossian Sars

An account of the Crustacea of Norway,
With short descriptions and figures of all the species - Vol. 1

ISBN/EAN: 9783337724009

Printed in Europe, USA, Canada, Australia, Japan

Cover: Foto ©ninafisch / pixelio.de

More available books at **www.hansebooks.com**

AN ACCOUNT

OF THE

CRUSTACEA

OF

NORWAY

AN ACCOUNT

OF THE

CRUSTACEA

OF

NORWAY,

WITH SHORT DESCRIPTIONS AND FIGURES OF ALL THE SPECIES

BY

G. O. SARS

PROFESSOR AT THE UNIVERSITY OF CHRISTIANIA

Vol 1.

AMPHIPODA

(PLATES.)

CHRISTIANIA AND COPENHAGEN

ALB. CAMMERMEYERS FORLAG

(LARS SWANSTRØM)

1895

LIST OF PLATES.

In all the plates the same letters bear the same homological relation, which has been explained in pages 3 & 4.

Plate 1.
Gammarus locusta Lin. (as type of an Amphipod).

Plate 2.
Hyperia galba, (Mont.) ♀.

Plate 3.
1. Hyperia galba, (Mont.) ♂.
2 Hyperia medusarum, (Müll.) ♀.

Plate 4.
Hyperoche tauriformis, (Sp. Bate) (see Appendix).

Plate 5.
1. Parathemisto oblivia, (Krøyer).
2. Euthemisto compressa, (Goës,.

Plate 6.
1. Euthemisto libellula, (Mandt.).
2. Euthemisto crassicornis (Krøyer) (see Appendix)

Plate 7.
Tryphæna Malmi, (Boeck).

Plate 8.
Scina borealis, G. O. Sars.

Plate 9.
Talitrus locusta, (Pallas).

Plate 10.
Orchestia littorea (Mont.).

Plate 11.
1. Hyale Nilssoni, (Rathke).
2. Hyale lubbockiana, (Sp. Bate).

Plate 12.
Trischizostoma Raschi, Boeck.

Plate 13.
1. Normanion quadrimanus, (Sp. Bate) (see Appendix).
2. Cheirimedon latimanus, G. O. Sars.

Plate 14.
1. Opisa Eschrichti, (Krøyer).
2. Acidostoma obesum, (Sp. Bate).

Plate 15.
Ichnopus spinicornis, Boeck.

Plate 16.
1. Lysianax Costæ, (M.-Edw.) (see Appendix).
2. Socarnes Vahli, (Krøyer).

Plate 17:
1. Ambasia Danielsseni, Boeck.
2. Aristias neglectus, Hansen (see Appendix).

Plate 18.
1. Aristias tumidus, (Krøyer)
2. Lysianella petalocera, G. O. Sars.

Plate 19.
1. Callisoma crenata, Sp. Bate.
2. Callisoma Krøyeri, (Bruzel.)

Plate 20.
Hippomedon denticulatus, (Sp. Bate)

Plate 21.
1. Hippomedon propinquus, G. O. Sars
2. Hippomedon Holbolli, (Krøyer).

Plate 22.
Orchomene Batei, G. O. Sars.

Plate 23.
1. Orchomene serratus, Boeck.
2. Orchomene crispatus, (Goes).
3. Orchomene pectinatus, G. O. Sars.

Plate 24.
1. Orchomenella minuta, (Krøyer).
2. Orchomenella pinguis, (Boeck
2. Nannonyx Goesii. (Boeck).

Plate 25.
1. Orchomene amblyops, G. O. Sars.
2. Orchomenella nana. (Krøyer) see Appendix).

Plate 26.
1. Orchomenella grønlandica, (Hansen.
2. Orchomenopsis obtusa G. O. Sars.

Plate 27.
1. Tryphosa Sarsi (Bonnier) (see Appendix)
2. Tryphosa Horringii Boeck

Plate 28
1. Tryphosa angulata, G. O. Sars.
2. Tryphosa nanoides, (Lilljeb.).
3. Tryphosites longipes (Sp. Bate) ♀.

Plate 29.
1. Tryphosites longipes. (Sp. Bate) ♂.
2 Pseudotryphosa umbonata, G. O. Sars.

Plate 30.
Euryporeia gryllus, (Mandt) (see text).

Plate 31.
Anonyx lagena Krøyer (see Appendix).

Plate 32
1. Anonyx Lilljeborgii, Boeck.
2. Hoplonyx cicada (Fabr.)

Plate 33
1. Hoplonyx similis, G. O. Sars.
2. Hoplonyx acutus. G. O. Sars.
3. Hoplonyx albidus, G. O. Sars.

Plate 34.
1. Hoplonyx leucophthalmus. G. O. Sars.
2. Centromedon pumilus (Lilljeb.

Plate 35.
1. Hoplonyx cæculus, G. O. Sars
2. Alibrotus littoralis (Krøyer

Plate 36.
1. Onesimus Edwardsii, Krøyer).
2 Onesimus Normani (Schneider).

Plate 37.
1 Onesimus plautus (Krøyer)
2. Chironesimus Debruynii. Boeck)

Plate 38
1. Menigrates obtusifrons. Boeck.
2. Lepidepecreum carinatum, Sp. Bate ♂.

Plate 39
1. Lepidepecreum carinatum, Sp. Bate ♂.
2. Lepidepecreum umbo, (Goes).

Plate 40.
1. Euonyx chelatus Norman
2. Kerguelenia borealis, G. O. Sars.

Plate 41.
1. Pontoporeia femorata, Krøyer.
2. Pontoporeia affinis Bruzelius.

Plate 42.
Priscilla armata, Boeck.

Plate 43.
Bathyporeia norvegica, G. O. Sars.

Plate 44.
1. Bathyporeia pelagica, Sp Bate.
2. Bathyporeia Robertsoni, Sp. Bate ♂.

Plate 45.
1. Bathyporeia gracilis, G. O. Sars.
1. Bathyporeia pilosa, Lindstrøm

Plate 46.
Haustorius arenarius. (Slabber)

Plate 47.
Urothoe norvegica, Boeck

Plate 48.
Argissa typica. Boeck.

Plate 49.
Phoxocephalus Holbølli, (Krøyer).

Plate 50.
Leptophoxus falcatus, G. O. Sars.

Plate 51.
Paraphoxus oculatus, G. O. Sars

Plate 52
Harpinia plumosa, (Krøyer).

Plate 53.
1. Harpinia neglecta, G. O. Sars.
2. Harpinia pectinata, G. O. Sars.

Plate 54.
1. Harpinia serrata, G. O. Sars.
2. Harpinia propinqua, G. O. Sars.
3. Harpinia mucronata, G. O. Sars.

Plate 55.
1. Harpinia truncata, G. O. Sars.
2. Harpinia crenulata, Boeck.

Plate 56.
1. Harpinia abyssi, G. O. Sars.
2. Harpinia lævis, G. O. Sars.

Plate 57.
Ampelisca typica, Sp. Bate.

Plate 58.
1. Ampelisca tenuicornis, Lilljeb.
2. Ampelisca assimilis.

Plate 59.
1. Ampelisca lævigata, Lilljeb.
2. Ampelisca gibba, G. O. Sars

Plate 60.
1. Ampelisca macrocephala, Lilljeb.
2. Ampelisca spinipes, Boeck.

Plate 61.
1. Ampelisca Eschrichti, Krøyer
2. Ampelisca odontoplax, G. O. Sars.

Plate 62.
1. Ampelisca æquicornis, Bruzel.
2. Ampelisca anomala, G. O. Sars.

Plate 63.
1. Ampelisca amblyops, G. O. Sars.
2. Ampelisca pusilla, G. O. Sars.

Plate 64.
Byblis Gaimardi, (Krøyer).

Plate 65.
1. Byblis longicornis, G. O. Sars.
2. Byblis affinis, G. O. Sars.
3. Byblis erythrops G. O. Sars.

Plate 66.
1. Byblis crassicornis, Metzger.
2. Byblis abyssi, G. O. Sars
3. Byblis minuticornis, G. O. Sars.

Plate 67.
Haploops tubicola, Lilljeb.

Plate 68.
1. Haploops setosa, Boeck.
2. Haploops robusta. G. O. Sars.

Plate 69.
Stegocephalus inflatus, Krøyer.

Plate 70.
1. Stegocephalus similis, G. O. Sars.
2. Stegocephaloides christianiensis, (Boeck).
3. Stegocephaloides auratus, G. O. Sars.

Plate 71.
1. Aspidopleurus gibbosus, G. O. Sars.
2. Andania abyssi, Boeck.

Plate 72.
1. Andania abyssi. Boeck (contin.).
2. Andaniopsis nordlandica, (Boeck)
3. Andaniella pectinata, G. O. Sars.

Plate 73.
Astyra abyssi, Boeck.

Plate 74.
Amphilochus manudens, Sp. Bate.

Plate 75.
1. Amphilochus tenuimanus. Boeck.
2. Amphilochoides Boeckii G. O. Sars (see Appendix).

Plate 76.
1. Amphilochoides odontonyx, (Boeck) (see Appendix).
2. Gitanopsis bispinosa, (Boeck).

Plate 77.
1. Gitanopsis inermis, G. O. Sars.
2. Gitanopsis arctica, G. O. Sars.

Plate 78.
1. Gitana Sarsii. Boeck.
2. Gitana abyssicola, G. O. Sars.

Plate 79.
1 Gitana rostrata Boeck.
2. Stegoplax longirostris, G. O. Sars.

Plate 80.
Stenothoe marina, (Sp. Bate).

Plate 81
1. Stenothoë microps, G. O. Sars.
2. Stenothoë tenella, G. O. Sars.

Plate 82
1. Stenothoë monoculoides, (Mont).
2. Stenothoë brevicornis, G. O. Sars.

Plate 83.
Stenothoë megachcir (Boeck.

Plate 84
Probolium gregarium, G. O. Sars.

Plate 85
Probolium calcaratum, G. O. Sars.

Plate 86.
Metopa Alderi, (Sp. Bate)

Plate 87
Metopa spectabilis, G. O. Sars.

Plate 88
Metopa Boeckii. G. O. Sars

Plate 89.
1 Metopa borealis, G. O. Sars.
2. Metopa rubrovittata, G. O. Sars

Plate 90.
1. Metopa pusilla, G. O. Sars.
2. Metopa longicornis Boeck.

Plate 91.
1. Metopa tenuimana G. O. Sars
2. Metopa affinis. Boeck.

Plate 92.
1 Metopa Bruzelii Goës.
2 Metopa sinuata, G. O. Sars

Plate 93.
1 Metopa propinqua, G. O. Sars
2. Metopa leptocarpa G. O. Sars

Plate 94.
1. Metopa Solsbergi Schneider
2 Metopa invalida G. O. Sars.

Plate 95.
Metopa pollexiens. Sp. Bate.

Plate 95.
Metopa robusta G. O. Sars.
2 Metopa pulchra G. O. Sars

Plate 97.
1 Metopa longimana, Boeck.
2 Metopa neglecta, Hansen.

Plate 98.
1 Metopa nasuta, Boeck.
2 Cressa dubia Sp. Bate

Plate 99.
1 Cressa dubia, (Sp Bate) (contin.)
2. Cressa minuta Boeck.

Plate 100.
Leucothoe spinicarpa Abildg) (see text

Plate 101
1. Leucothoe spinicarpa (Abildg (contin
2. Leucothoë Lilljeborgii, Boeck (see text

Plate 102.
Œdiceros sagittatus Kroyer.

Plate 103.
1 Œdiceros borealis Boeck.
2. Paroediceros lynceus, (M. Sars.

Plate 104
1. Paroediceros lynceus (M. Sars) (contin)
2. Paroediceros propinquus, (Goës.

Plate 105.
Monoculodes carinatus. Sp. Bate.

Plate 106.
1. Monoculodes tessellatus, Schneider.
2. Monoculodes borealis, Boeck.
3. Monoculodes pallidus, G. O. Sars.

Plate 107.
1 Monoculodes norvegicus. Boeck.
2 Monoculodes falcatus, G. O. Sars.
3. Monoculodes tuberculatus Boeck.

Plate 108
1. Monoculodes latimanus (Goës.
2. Monoculodes Kroyeri. Boeck.
3 Monoculodes longirostris, (Goës

Plate 109.
1 Monoculodes Packardi, Boeck.
2 Monoculodes tenuirostratus, Boeck.

Plate 110.
1. Monoculopsis longicornis, (Boeck.
2 Perioculodes longimanus. (Sp. Bate)

IX

Plate 111.
1. Perioculodes longimanus, (Sp. Bate) (contin.)
2 Pontocrates arcticus. G. O. Sars (see Appendix).

Plate 112.
1. Synchelidium brevicarpum. (Sp. Bate).
2. Synchelidium haplocheles, (Grube).

Plate 113.
1 Synchelidium intermedium, G. O. Sars.
2. Halicreion longicaudatus. Boeck.

Plate 114.
Œdiceropsis brevicornis, Lilljeb.

Plate 115
Halimedon Mülleri, Boeck.

Plate 116.
1. Halimedon acutifrons, G. O. Sars.
2. Halimedon megalops, G. O. Sars.
3. Halimedon brevicalcar, (Goës).

Plate 117.
Bathymedon longimanus, (Boeck).

Plate 118
1 Bathymedon Saussurei, (Boeck).
2. Bathymedon obtusifrons. (Hansen)

Plate 119.
Aceros phyllonyx, (M. Sars).

Plate 120.
1. Aceros phyllonyx, (M. Sars) ♂.
2. Acceroides latipes, G. O. Sars (see text).

Plate 121.
Pleustes panoplus. (Kroyer).

Plate 122.
1. Paramphithoë pulchella, (Kroyer).
2. Paramphithoë Boeckii, Hansen.

Plate 123.
1. Paramphithoë bicuspis, (Kroyer).
2. Paramphithoë monocuspis, G. O. Sars.

Plate 124.
1. Paramphithoë assimilis, G. O. Sars.
2. Paramphithoë brevicornis, G. O. Sars

Plate 125.
1. Stenopleustes Malmgreni, (Boeck).
2. Stenopleustes nodifer, G. O. Sars

b Crustacea.

Plate 126.
1. Parapleustes glaber. (Boeck).
2. Parapleustes pulchellus, G. O. Sars.

Plate 127.
Parapleustes latipes, (M. Sars).

Plate 128.
Epimeria cornigera. (Fabr.)

Plate 129.
1. Epimeria parasitica, (M. Sars).
2. Epimeria tuberculata, G. O. Sars.
3. Epimeria loricata, G. O. Sars

Plate 130.
Acanthozone cuspidata, (Lepechin).

Plate 131.
1. Acanthonotosoma serratum, (Fabr.)
2. Acanthonotosoma cristatum, (Owen).

Plate 132.
Iphimedia obesa, Rathke

Plate 133.
1. Iphimedia minuta, G. O. Sars.
2. Odius carinatus, (Sp. Bate).

Plate 134.
Laphystius sturionis, Kroyer.

Plate 135.
Laphystiopsis planifrons, G. O. Sars.

Plate 136.
Syrrhoë crenulata, Goës.

Plate 137.
Syrrhoites serrata, G. O. Sars.

Plate 138.
Bruzelia typica, Boeck.

Plate 139.
1. Bruzelia typica, Boeck (contin.)
2. Bruzelia tuberculata, G. O. Sars.

Plate 140.
Tiron acanthurus, Lilljeb.

Plate 141.
Pardalisca cuspidata, Kroyer.

Plate 142
1. Pardalisca cuspidata, Kroyer contin
2. Pardalisca tenuipes G. O. Sars

Plate 143.
1. Pardalisca abyssi, Boeck
2. Pardaliscella Boecki, Malm

Plate 144.
Nicippe tumida, Bruzelius.

Plate 145.
1. Nicippe tumida, Bruzel. (contin.)
2. Halice abyssi, Boeck

Plate 146.
Eusirus cuspidatus, Kröyer.

Plate 147
1. Eusirus propinquus, G. O. Sars.
2. Eusirus minutus, G. O. Sars

Plate 148.
1. Eusirus longipes, Boeck.
2. Eusirus leptocarpus, G. O. Sars

Plate 149.
Rhachotropis aculeata, Lepechin

Plate 150.
Rhachotropis Helleri, Boeck

Plate 151.
1. Rhachotropis macropus, G. O. Sars
2. Rhachotropis leucophthalma, G. O. Sars

Plate 152.
Rhachotropis inflata, G. O. Sars (see Appendix

Plate 153.
Halirageides inermis, G. O. Sars.

Plate 154
Halirages fulvocinctus, M. Sars

Plate 155.
1. Apherusa bispinosa, (Sp. Bate
2. Apherusa borealis, Boeck).

Plate 156.
1. Apherusa tridentata, Bruzel.)
2. Apherusa Clevei, G. O. Sars

Plate 157.
1. Acidostoma Jurinei, M. Edw.)
2. Callisoma Krøyeri, Zaddach).

Plate 158.
Callisoma crenata, Kröyer

Plate 159.
Pontogeneia inermis, Kröyer.

Plate 160.
Laothoe Meinerti, Boeck (see text).

Plate 161.
Amphithopsis longicaudata, Boeck

Plate 162.
Leptamphopus longimanus (Boeck).

Plate 163.
Paratylus Swammerdami (M. Edw.

Plate 164.
1. Paratylus uncinatus, G. O. Sars (see Appendix).
2. Paratylus vedlomensis, Sp. Bate).

Plate 165.
1. Paratylus Smitti, Goes.
2. Paratylus nordlandicus, Boeck)

Plate 166.
1. Atylus carinatus, (Fabr.)
2. Dexamine spinosa, (Mont.) ♂.

Plate 167.
Dexamine spinosa, Mont., ♀.

Plate 168.
1. Dexamine Thea, Boeck.
2. Tritaeta gibbosa, (Sp. Bate) ♀.

Plate 169.
Melphidippa spinosa, Goes

Plate 170.
1. Melphidippa macrura, G. O. Sars.
2. Melphidippa borealis, Boeck.

Plate 171.
Melphidippella macera, (Norman

Plate 172
Amathilla homari, (Fabr.) ♀.

Plate 173.
1. Amathilla homari, Fabr.) ♂.
2. Amathilla angulosa, (Rathke).

Plate 174.
Gammaracanthus relictus, G. O. Sars.

XI

Plate 175.
Gammarus marinus. Leach.

Plate 176.
1. Gammarus locusta, (Lin.)
2. Gammarus campylops, Leach.

Plate 177.
1. Gammarus Duebeni, Lilljeb.
2. Gammarus pulex, (Lin.).

Plate 178.
Pallasiella quadrispinosa, (Esm.)

Plate 179.
Melita palmata, (Mont.).

Plate 180.
1. Melita obtusata, (Mont.).
2. Melita pellucida. G. O. Sars

Plate 181.
1. Melita dentata, (Krøyer).
2. Eriopisa elongata, (Bruzel.).

Plate 182.
1. Mæra Othonis, (M.-Edw.).
2. Mæra Lovéni, (Bruzel.).

Plate 183.
Elasmopus rapax, (M.-Edw.).

Plate 184.
Cheirocratus Sundewalli, (Rathke) ♀

Plate 185.
1. Cheirocratus Sundewalli, (Rathke) ♂.
2. Cheirocratus robustus, G. O. Sars ♂

Plate 186.
1. Cheirocratus intermedius, G. O. Sars ♂.
2. Cheirocratus assimilis, (Lilljeb.) ♂.

Plate 187.
Lilljeborgia pallida, Sp. Bate.

Plate 188.
1. Lilljeborgia Kinahani, (Sp. Bate).
2. Lilljeborgia macronyx, G. O. Sars

Plate 189.
Lilljeborgia fissicornis, (M. Sars).

Plate 190.
Idunella æquicornis, G. O. Sars.

Plate 191.
Microdeutopus anomalus, (Rathke).

Plate 192.
1. Microdeutopus danmoniensis, (Sp. Bate) (see text).
2. Microdeutopus gryllotalpa, Costa.

Plate 193.
Aora gracilis, Sp. Bate.

Plate 194.
Autonoe Websteri, Sp. Bate).

Plate 195.
1. Autonoe longipes, (Lilljeb.).
2. Autonoe megacheir. G. O. Sars.

Plate 196.
Protomedeia fasciata. Krøyer.

Plate 197.
Leptocheirus pilosus, Zaddach.

Plate 198.
Gammaropsis erythrophthalma, Lilljeborg.

Plate 199.
1. Gammaropsis melauops. G. O. Sars.
2. Gammaropsis nana, G. O. Sars,

Plate 200.
Megamphopus cornutus, Norman.

Plate 201.
Microprotopus maculatus, Norman.

Plate 202.
Photis Reinhardi. Krøyer.

Plate 203.
1. Photis longicaudata Sp. Bate).
2. Photis tenuicornis, G. O. Sars.

Plate 204.
Podoceropsis Sophiae, Boeck.

Plate 205.
Podoceropsis excavata. (Sp. Bate

Plate 206.
Amphithoe rubricata. (Mont.)

Plate 207.
Pleonexes gammaroides, Sp. Bate

Plate 208
Siuanpinthoe ronformata. Sp Bate.

Plate 209.
Ischyrocerus anguipes. Kroyer.

Plate 210.
1 Ischyrocerus minutus Liljeb.
2 Ischyrocerus megalops G. O Sars.

Plate 211
Ischyrocerus megacheir, (Boeck).

Plate 212
Podocerus falcatus, Mont)

Plate 213
1. Podocerus pusillus G. O. Sars.
2 Podocerus odontonyx G. O. Sars.

Plate 214.
Janassa capillata, (Rathke).

Plate 215.
Ericthonius abditus. (Templeton).

Plate 216
1. Erichthonius difformis, M.-Edw.
2. Erichthonius Hunteri Sp. Bate).

Plate 217
Cerapus crassicornis Sp. Bate)

Plate 218
1. Siphonoccetes Colletti. Boeck
2. Siphonoccetes pallidus. G. O Sars

Plate 219.
Corophium grossipes, (Lin.)

Plate 220
Corophium crassicorne. Bruzel.

Plate 221.
1. Corophium Bonelli, M.-Edw
2 Corophium affine. Bruzel.

Plate 222
Unciola leucopis (Kroyer

Plate 223.
Unciola planipes Norman.

Plate 224.
Neobule nematosa, (Boeck).

Plate 225.
Chelura terebrans Philippi.

Plate 226.
Laetmatophilus tuberculatus, Bruzel.

Plate 227.
1. Laetmatophilus armatus, (Norman).
2. Xenodice Frauenfeldti, Boeck

Plate 228.
Dulichia spinosissima Kroyer.

Plate 229.
Dulichia porrecta Sp. Bate.

Plate 230.
1. Dulichia monacantha, Metzger.
2. Dulichia curticauda, Boeck.

Plate 231.
1. Dulichia falcata, Sp. Bate.
2 Dulichia nordlandica, Boeck Q.

Plate 232.
1. Dulichia nordlandica, Boeck ♂.
2. Paradulichia typica, Boeck ♀.

Plate 233.
Phtisica marina, Slabber (see text).

Plate 234
1. Protella phasma, (Mont.).
2 Ægina echinata Boeck.

Plate 235.
1. Æginella spinosa, Boeck.
2 Pariambus typicus. (Kroyer) see text).

Plate 236.
Caprella linearis, (Lin.)

Plate 237.
1. Caprella septentrionalis, Kroyer.
2. Caprella punctata, Boeck.

Plate 238.
1. Caprella monocera, G. O. Sars.
2. Caprella Lovéni. Boeck.
3. Caprella æquilibra, Say.

Plate 239.
1. Caprella microtuberculata, G. O Sars.
2. Caprella ciliata, G. O. Sars.
3. Caprella acanthifera Leach.

XIII

Plate 240.
Paracyamus boopis, (Lütken) (see text).

Suppl. Plate I.
1. Normanion amblyops, G. O. Sars.
2. Aristias microps, G. O. Sars.

Suppl Plate II.
1. Aristias megalops, G. O. Sars.
2. Perrierella audouiniana, (Sp. Bate).

Suppl. Plate III.
1. Hippomedon robustus G. O. Sars
2. Orchomene Hanseni, Meinert.

Suppl. Plate IV.
1. Orchomene serrata, Boeck ♂.
2. Tryphosa compressa, G. O. Sars.

Suppl. Plate V.
Podoprionella norvegica, G. O. Sars.

Suppl. Plate VI.
1. Monoculodes Schneideri, G. O. Sars.
2. Pontocrates norvegicus, Boeck ♀.

Suppl. Plate VII.
1. Pontocrates norvegicus, Boeck ♂.
2 Pontocrates altamarinus, (Sp. Bate).

Suppl. Plate VIII.
1. Tritæta gibbosa, (Sp. Bate) ♂.
2. Dulichia Normani, G. O. Sars ♀.
3. Caprella punctata. Boeck ♂.

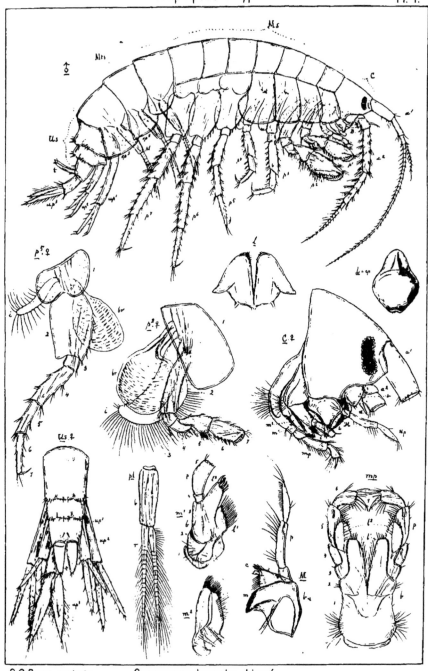

G.O.Sars autogr.   Gammarus locusta, Linné.

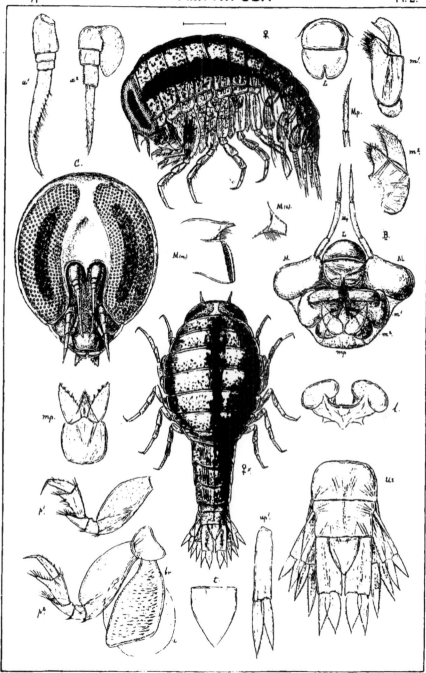

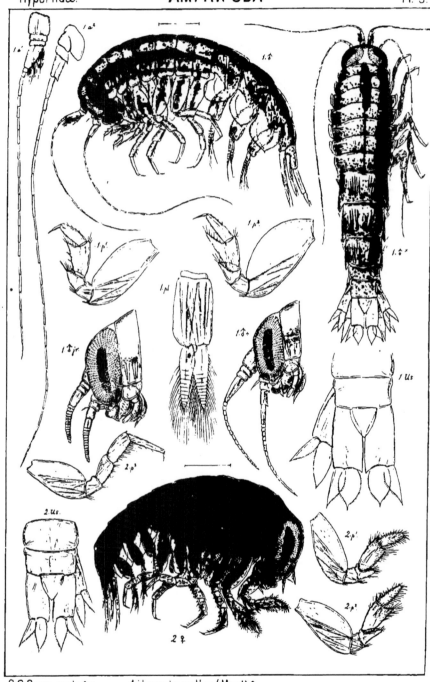

G.O.Sars autogr.
1. Hyperia galba, (Mont) ♂.
2. Hyperia medusarum, (Müll) ♀.

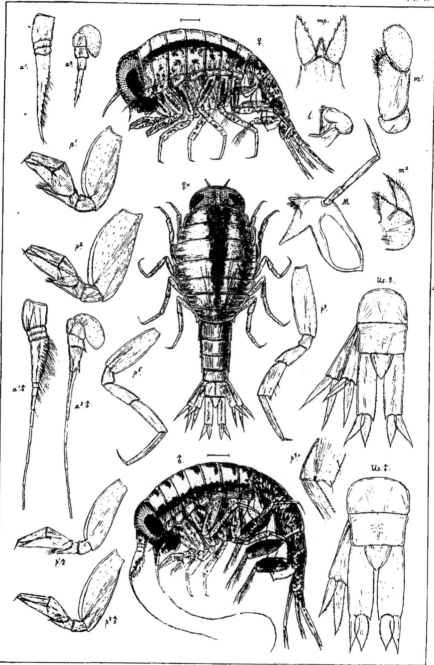

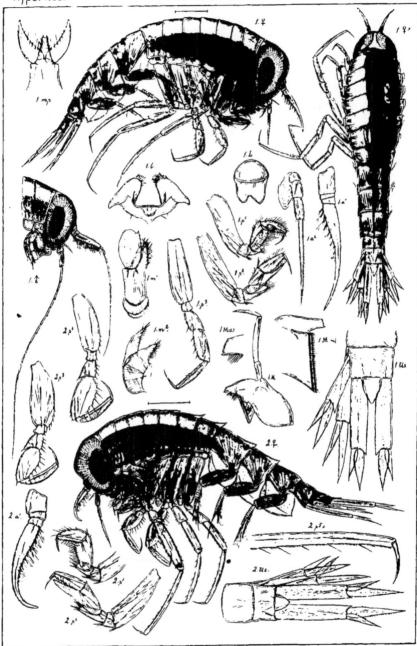

1. Parathemisto oblivia, (Kroeyer).
2. Euthemisto compressa, (Goës).

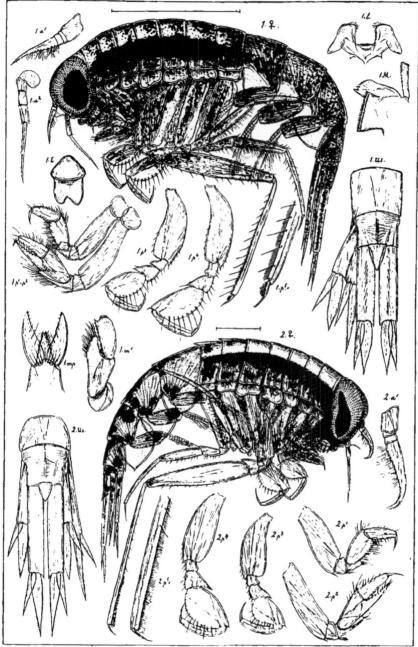

1. Euthemisto libellula, (Mandt).
2. Euthemisto bispinosa,(Boeck).

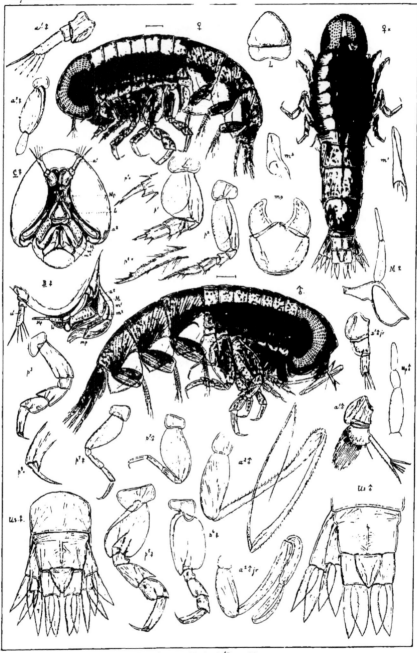

G.O.Sars autogr.   Tryphæna Malmi, (Boeck).

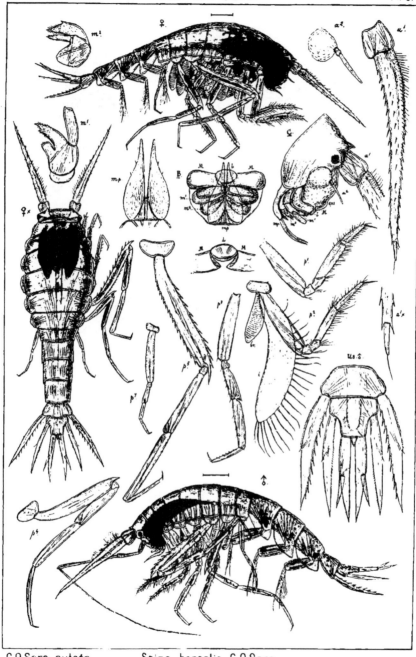

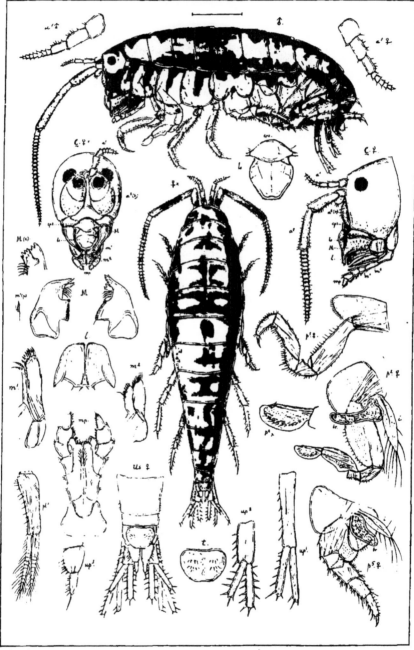

G.O.Sars autogr.   Talitrus locusta, (Pallas)

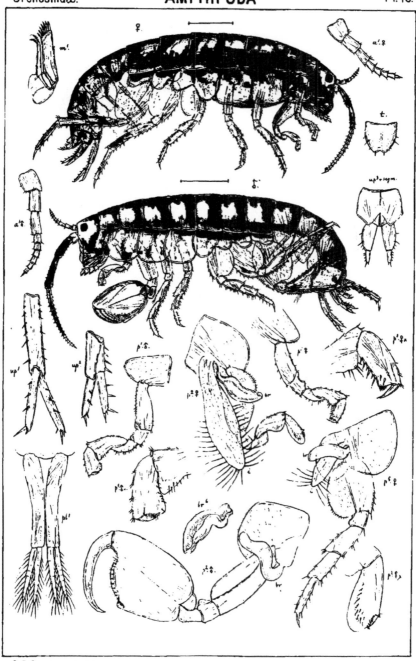

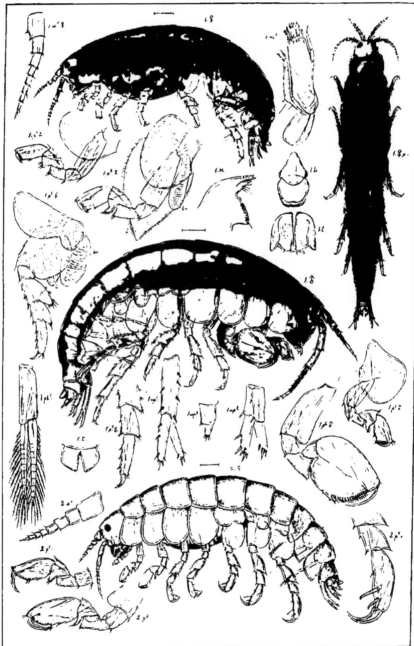

G.O Sars autogr.

1. Hyale Nilssoni, (Rathke).
2. Hyale lubbockiana, (Sp. Bate).

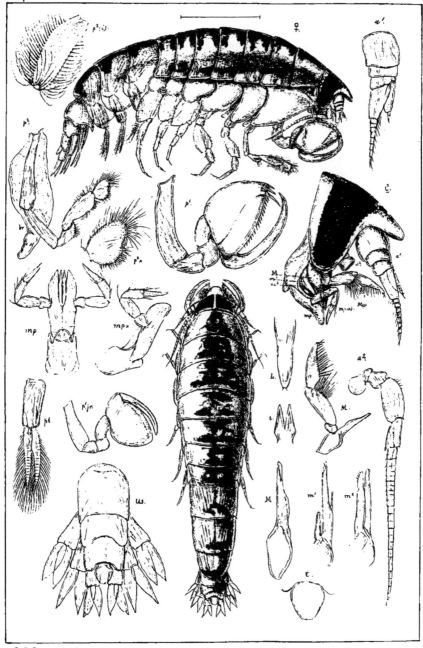

GOSars autogr.   Trischizostoma Raschi, Boeck.

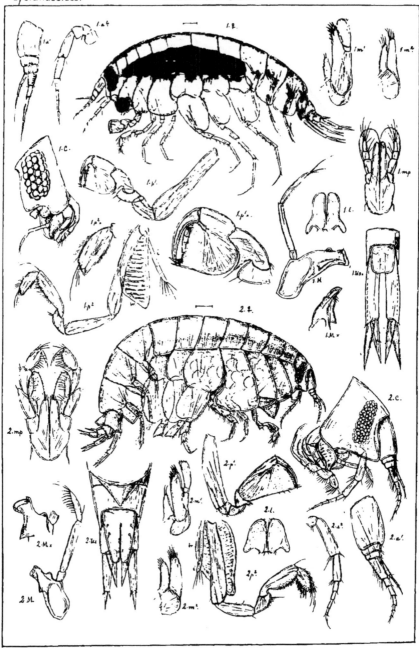

1. Normania qvadrimana, Sp. Bate.
2. Cheirómedon latimanus, G.O.Sars.

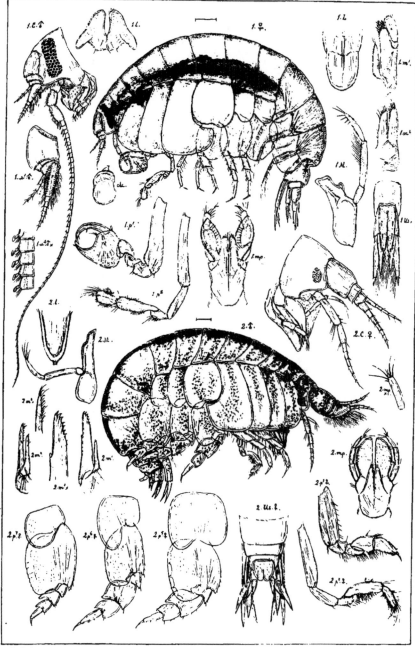

G.O.Sars autogr.

1.Opisa Eschrichti, Kröyer.
2.Acidostoma obesum, (Sp. Bate.)

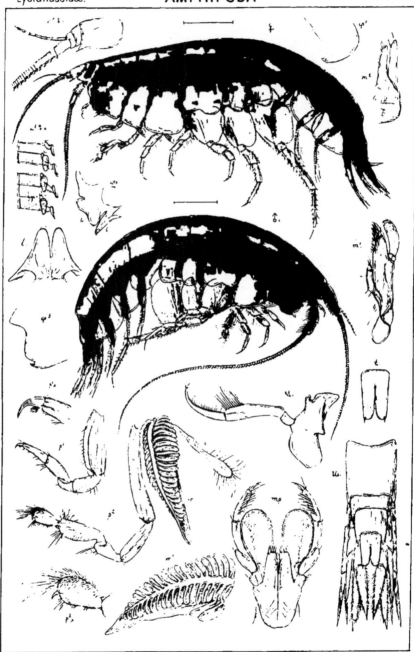

G.O.Sars autogr.   Ichnopus spinicornis, Boeck.

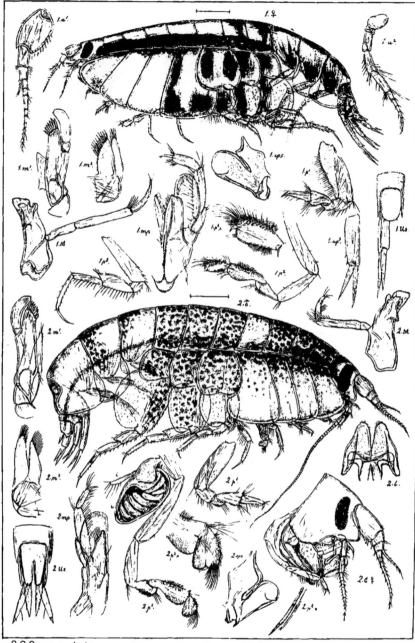

1. Lysianassa Costæ, M. Edw.
2. Socarnes Vahli, (Kröyer.)

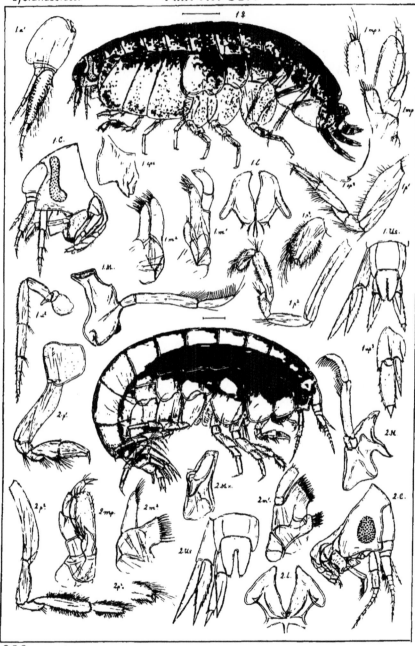

G.O Sars autogr. 1. Ambasia Danielsseni, Boeck.
2. Aristias audouinianus, (Sp. Bate).

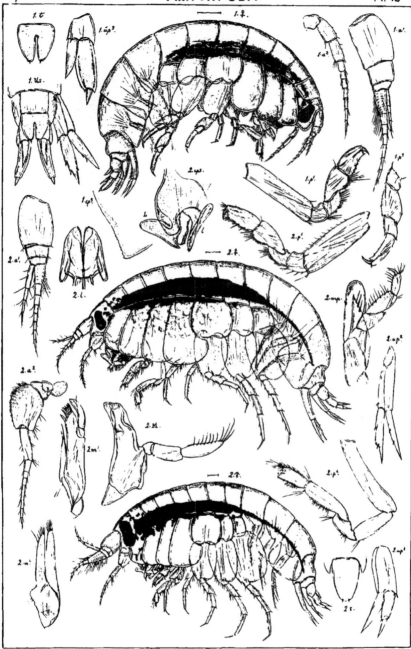

1. Aristias tumidus, (Kröyer).
2. Lysianella petalocera, G.O.Sars.

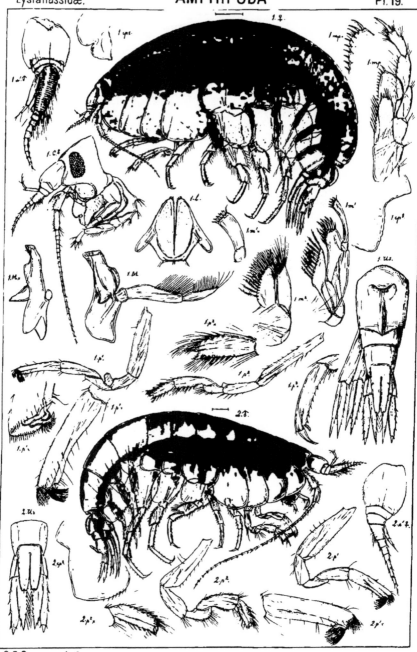

1. Callisoma crenata, Sp. Bate.
2. Callisoma Kröyeri, (Bruzelius).

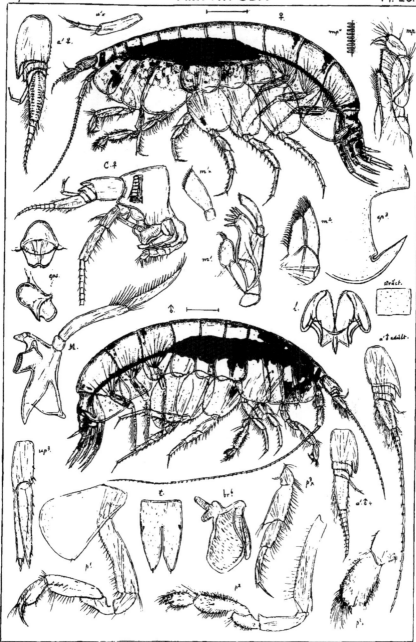

Hippomedon denticulatus, (Sp.Bate).

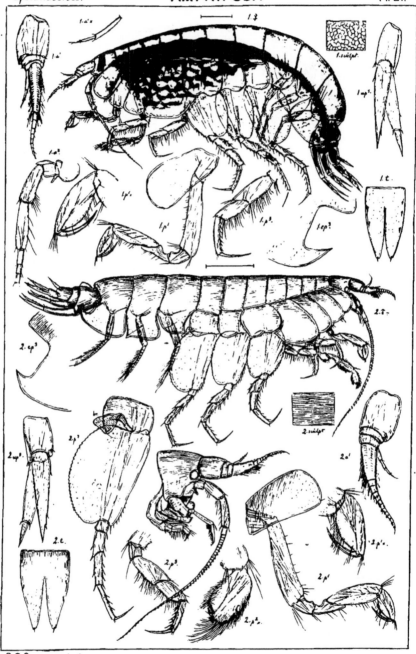

G.O.Sars autogr.

1. Hippomedon propinqvus, G.O.Sars.
2. Hippomedon Holbölli, (Kröyer).

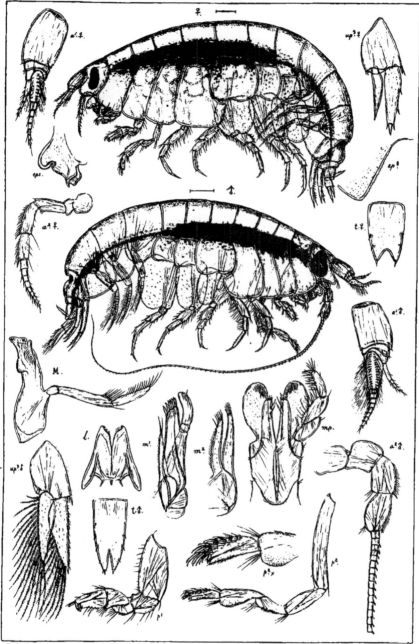

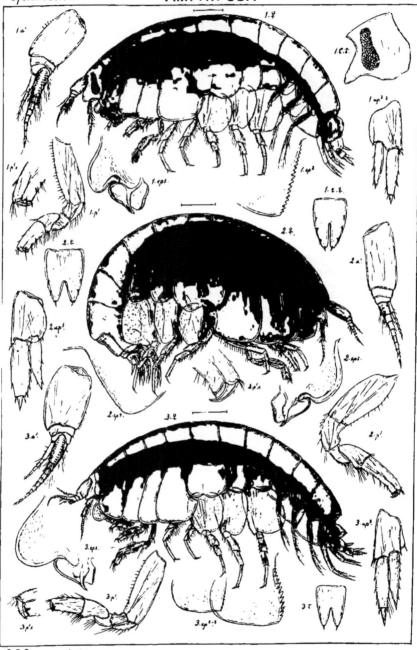

G.O.Sars autogr.

1. Orchomene serratus, Boeck.
2. Orchomene crispatus, (Goës).
3. Orchomene pectinatus, G.O.Sars.

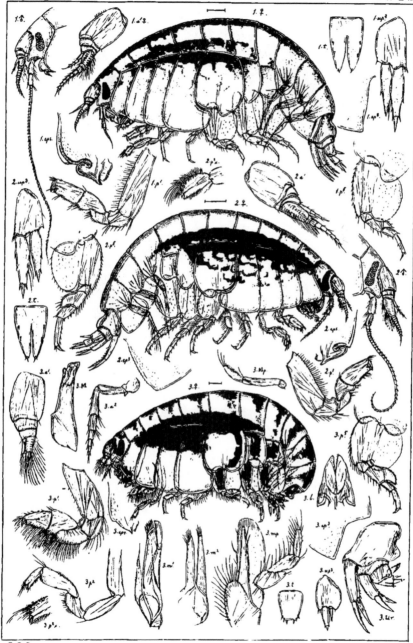

G O Sars autogr.

1. Orchomenella minuta (Kröyer).
2. Orchomenella pingvis (Boeck).
3. Nannonyx Goësil, (Boeck).

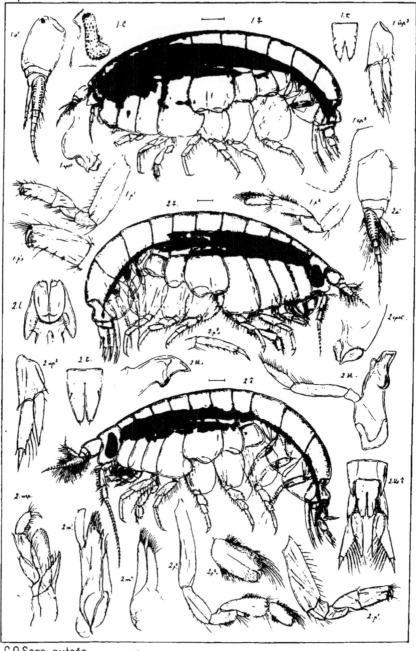

1. Orchomene amblyops, n.sp.
2. Orhomenella ciliata, G.O.Sars

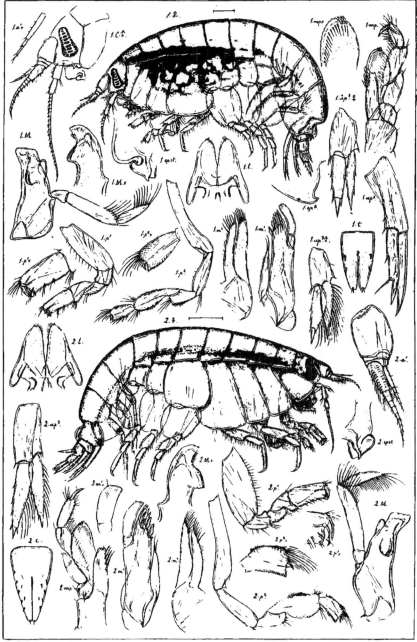

G.O.Sars autogr.

1. Orchomenella grönlandica, (Hansen).
2. Orchomenopsis obtusa, n. gen. & sp.

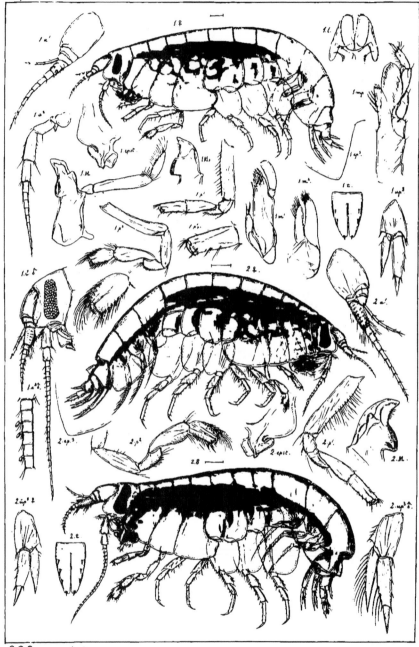

G.O.Sars autogr.

1. Tryphosa nana, (Kroyer).
2. Tryphosa Höringii, Boeck.

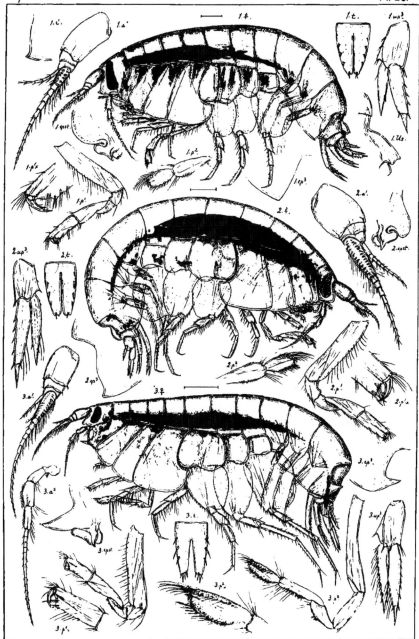

G.O.Sars autogr.　1. Tryphosa angulata, n. sp.
　　　　　　　　　2. Tryphosa nanoides, (Lilljeborg).
　　　　　　　　　3. Tryphosites longipes, (Sp. Bate).

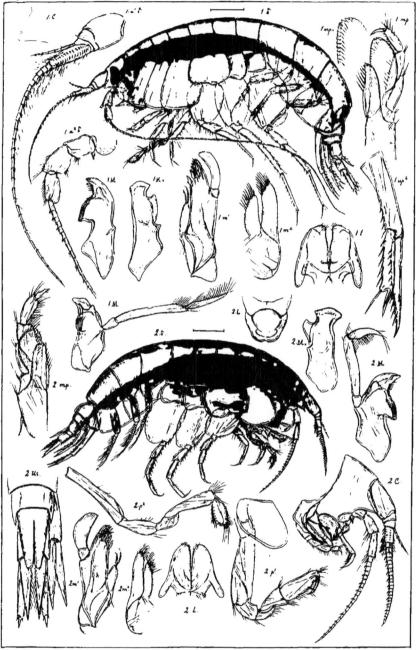

G.O.Sars autogr.   1. Tryphosites longipes, (Sp. Bate).
2. Pseudotryphosa umbonata, G.O.Sars.

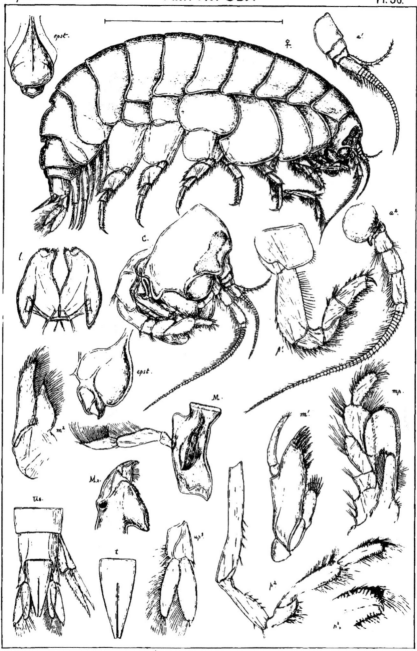

Eurytenes gryllus, (Mandt).

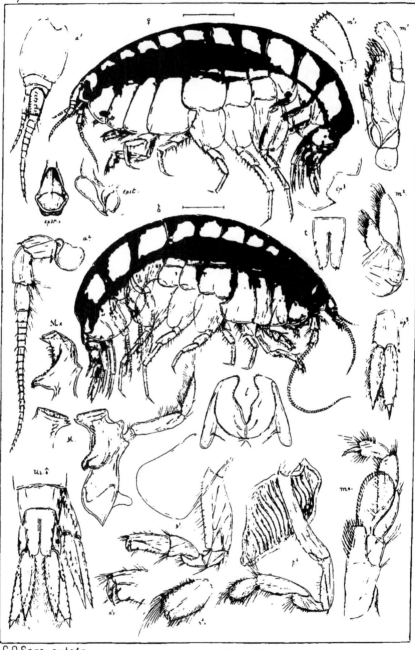

G.O.Sars autogr.   Anonyx nugax, (Phipps).

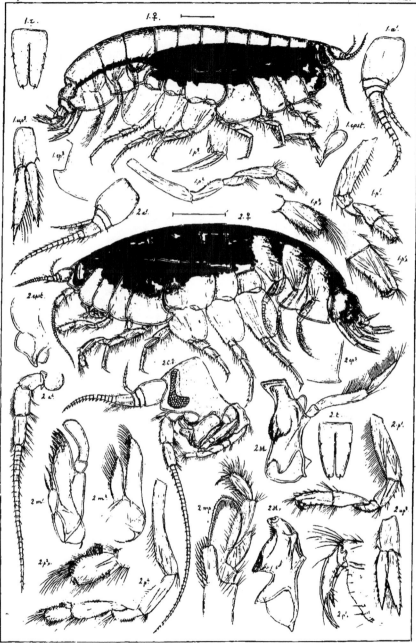

G.O.Sars autogr.
1. Anonyx Lilljeborgii, Boeck.
2. Hoplonyx cicada, (Fabr.).

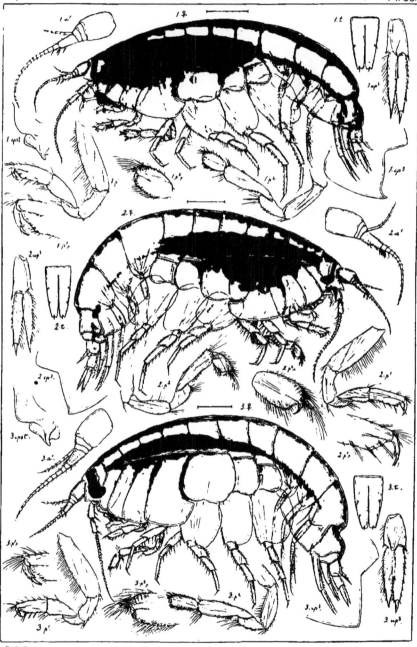

G.O.Sars autogr.
1. Hoplonyx similis, n. sp.
2. Hoplonyx acutus, n. sp.
3. Hoplonyx albidus, n. sp.

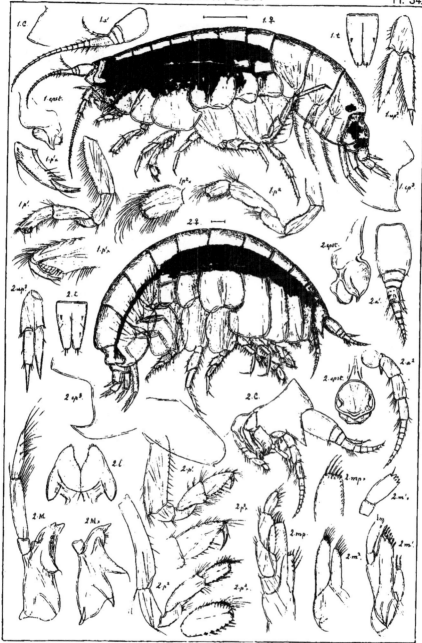

G.O.Sars autogr.   1.Hoplonyx leucophthalmus, n.sp.
2.Centromedon pumilus, (Lilljeborg).

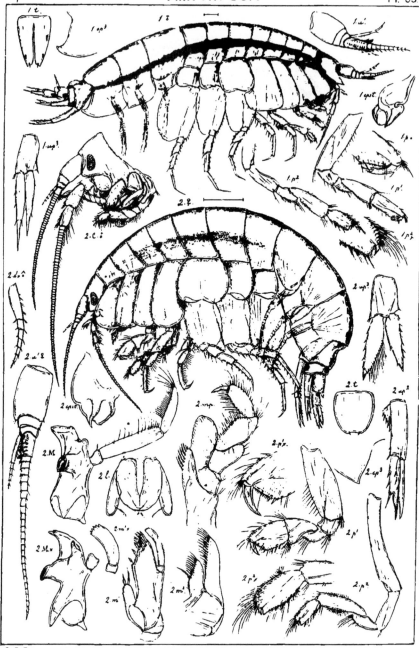

G.O.Sars autogr.

1. Hoplonyx caeculus. n. sp.
2. Alibrotus littoralis, (Kröyer).

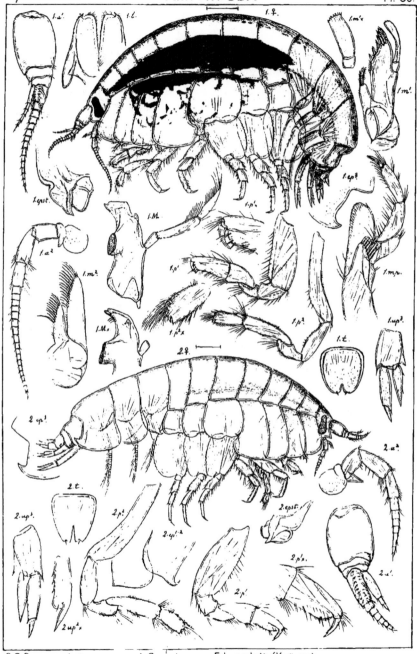

G.O Sars autogr.   1. Onesimus Edwardsii, (Kröyer).
2. Onesimus Normani, (Schneider).

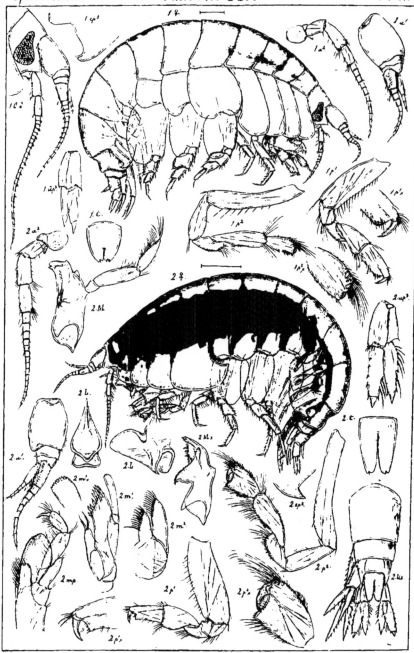

1. Onésimus plautus, (Kröyer).
2 Chironesimus Debruynli, (Hoek).

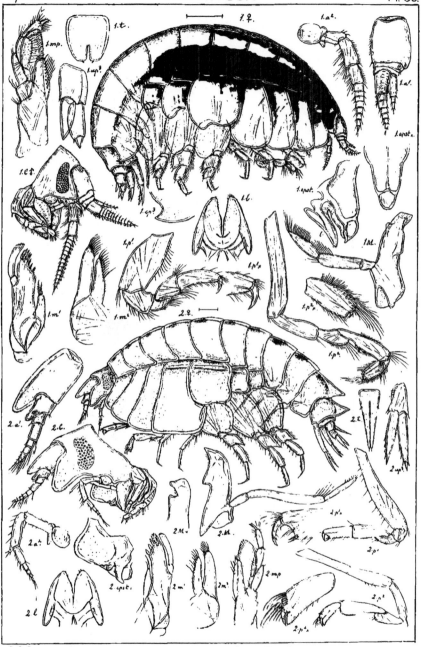

1. Menigrates obtusifrons, Boeck.
2. Lepidepecreum carinatum, Sp. Bate ♀.

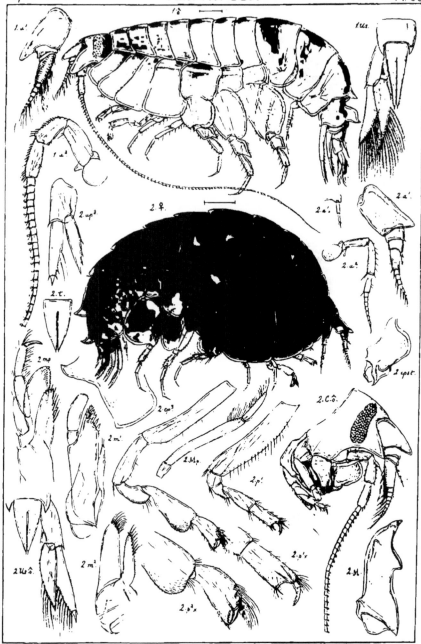

G O Sars autogr.

1. Lepidepecreum carinatum, Sp. Bate ♂.
2. Lepidepecreum umbo, (Goës).

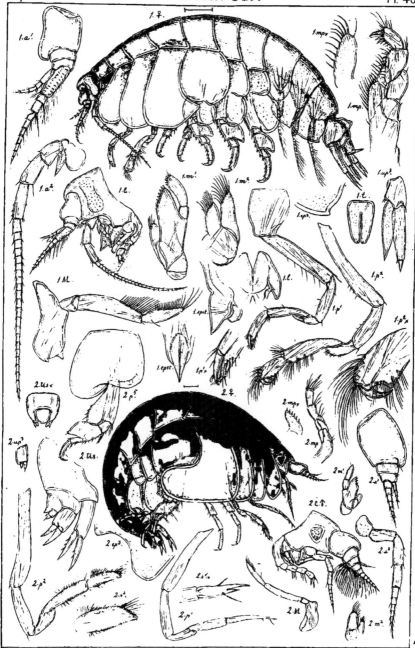

G.O.Sars autogr.

1. Euonyx chelatus, Norman.
2. Kerguelenia borealis, n. sp.

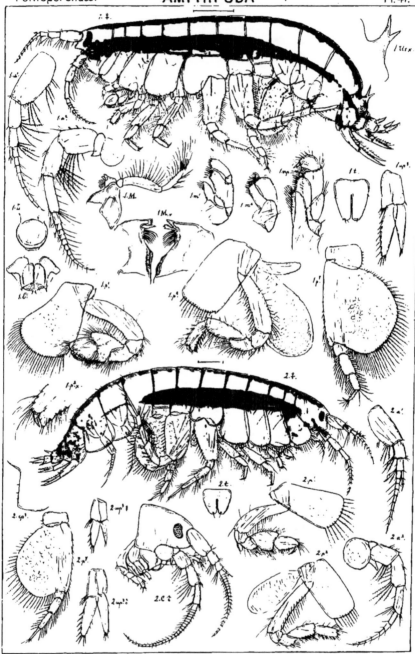

G.O Sars autogr.

1. Pontoporeia femorata, Kröyer.
2. Pontoporeia affinis, ~~Bruzelius~~.

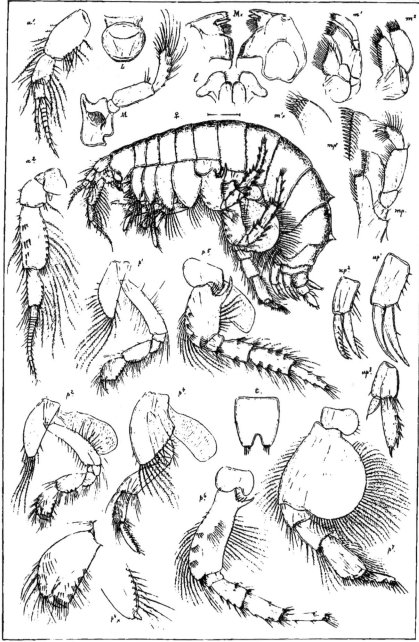

Priscilla armata, Boeck.

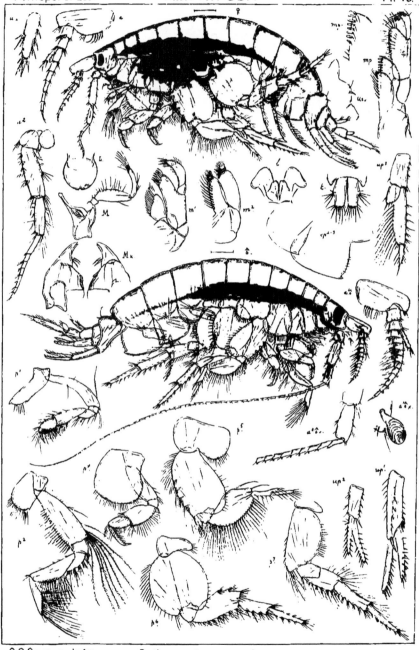

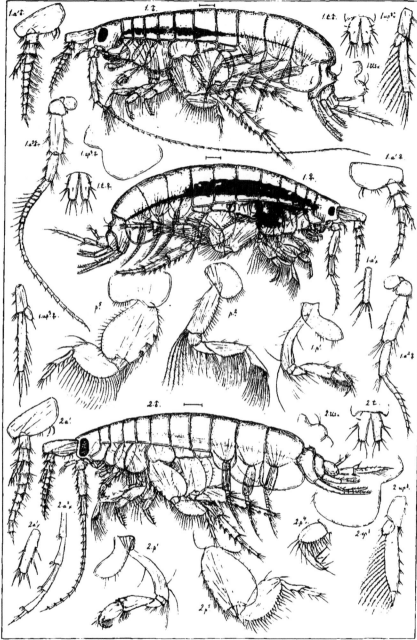

G.O.Sars autogr.　　1. Bathyporeia pelagica, Sp. Bate.
　　　　　　　　　　2. Bathyporeia Robertsonii, Sp. Bate.

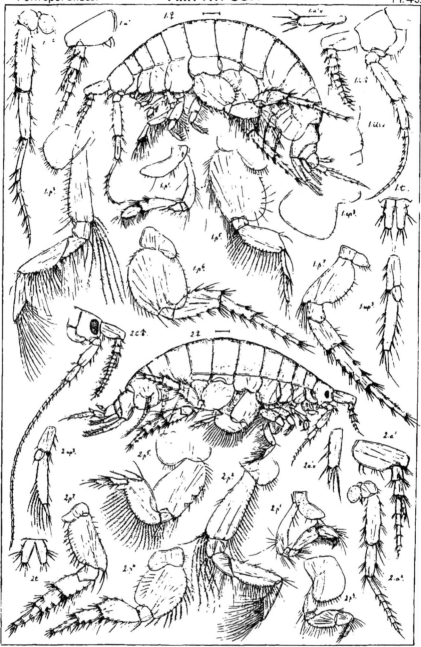

C.O.Sars autogr.   1. Bathyporeia gracilis, n.sp.
2. Bathyporeia pilosa, Lindström.

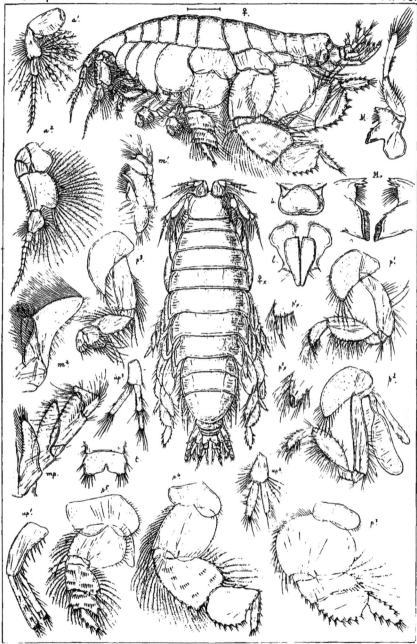

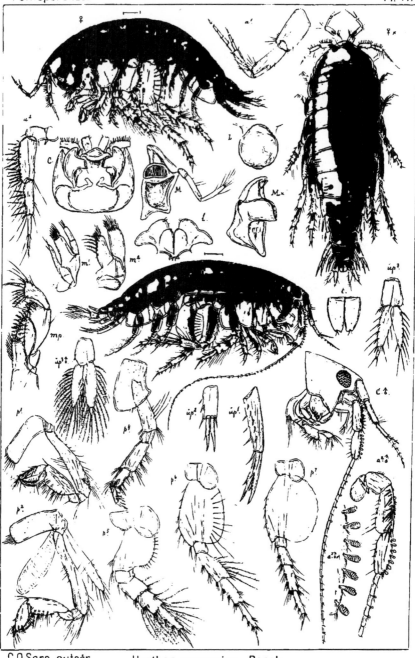

G.O.Sars autogr. Urothoe norvegica, Boeck.

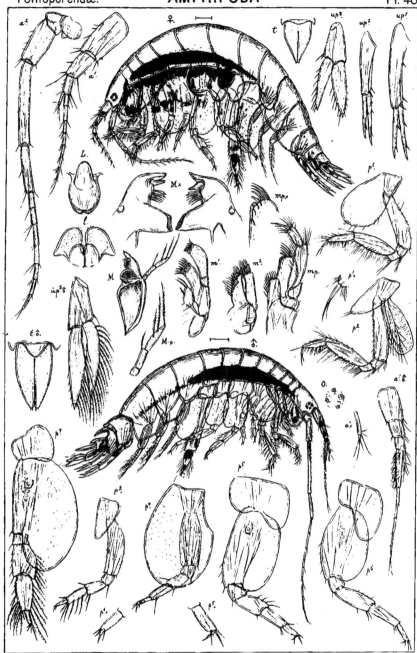

G.O.Sars autogr.   Argissa typica, Boeck.

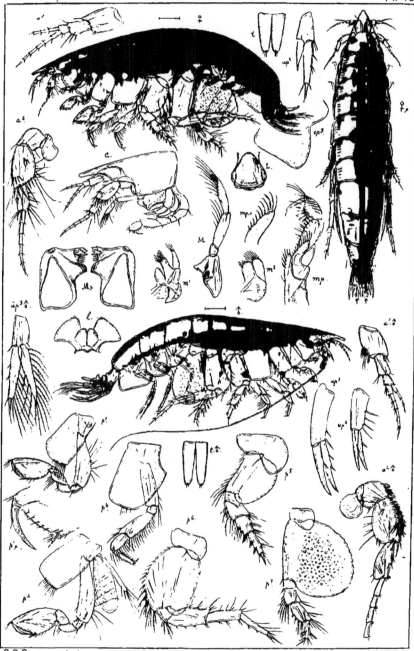

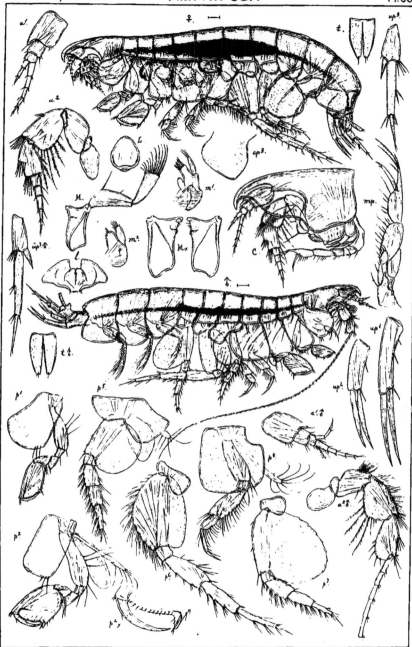

Leptophoxus falcatus, G.O.Sars.

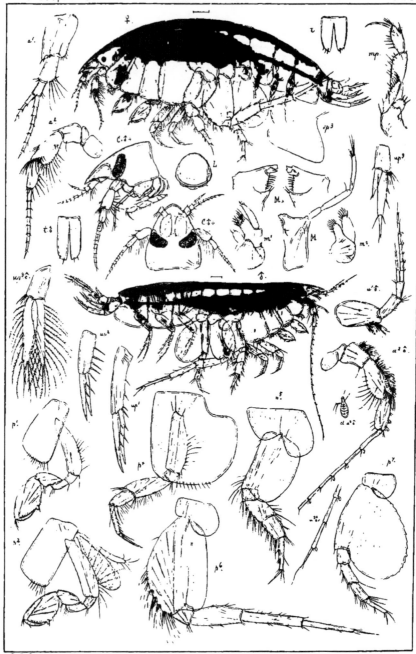

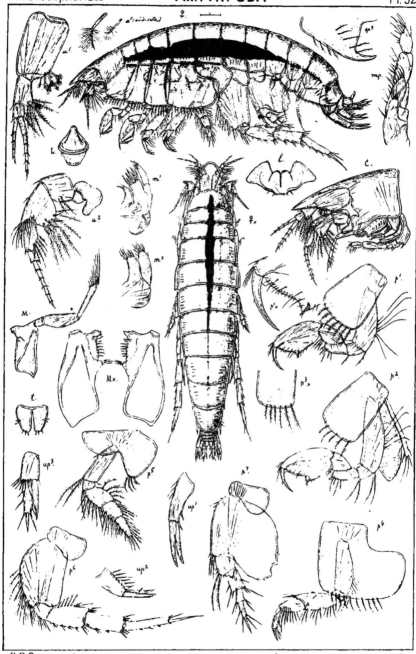

G.O.Sars autogr.   Harpinia plumosa (Kröyer).

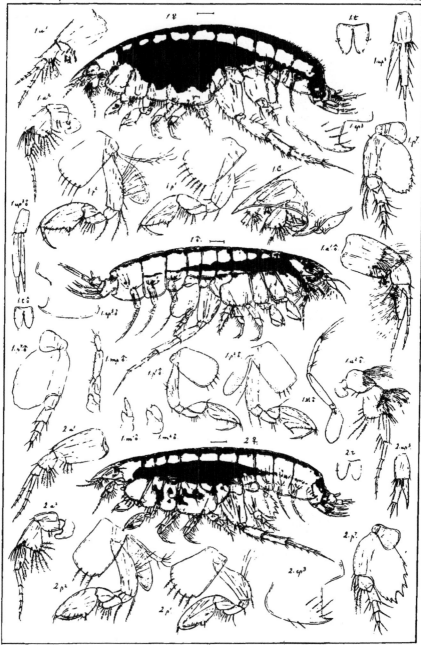

1. Harpinia neglecta, G.O.Sars.
2. Harpinia pectinata, n. sp.

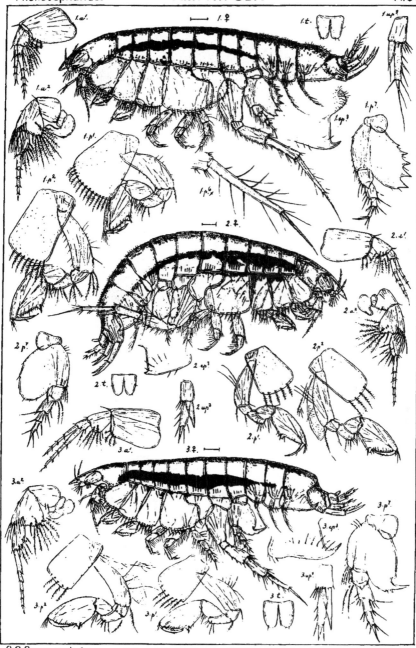

1. Harpinia serrata, G.O.Sars.
2. Harpinia propinqva, n. sp.
3. Harpinia mucronata, G.O.Sars.

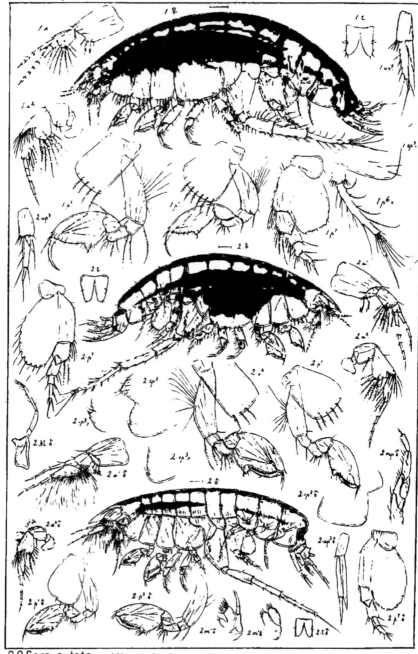

G.O.Sars autogr.   1.Harpinia truncata, n.sp.
                2.Harpinia creṅulata, ῀Boeck῀.

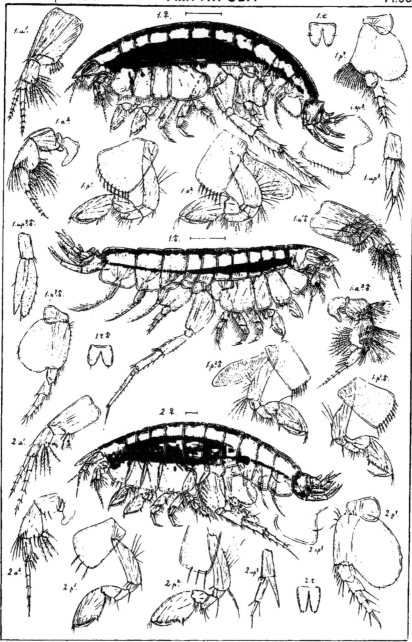

1. Harpinia abyssi, G.O.Sars.
2. Harpinia lævis n. sp.

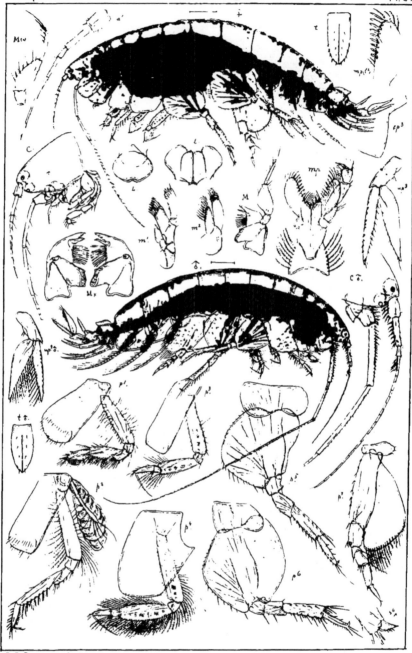

G.O.Sars autogr.   Ampelisca typica, Sp. Bate.

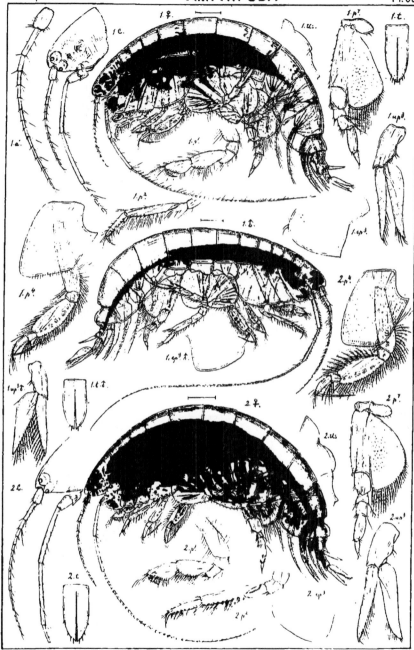

1. Ampelisca tenuicornis, Lilljeborg
2. Ampelisca assimilis, Boeck.
.4

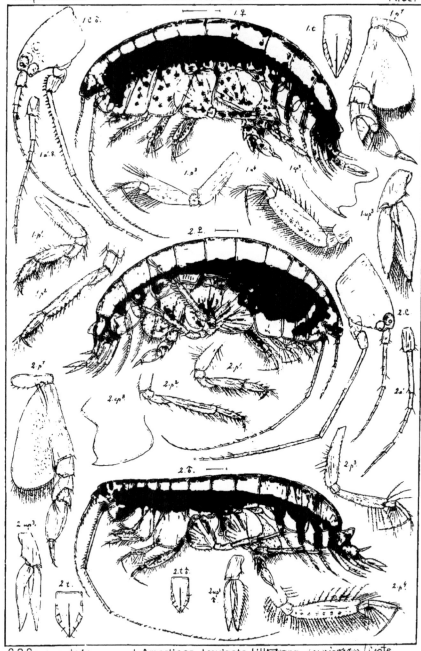

G.O Sars autogr.

1. Ampelisca laevigata, Lilljeborg.
2. Ampelisca gibba, G.O.Sars.

G O Sars autogr   1. Ampelisca macrocephala, Lilljeborg.
2. Ampelisca spinipes, Boeck.

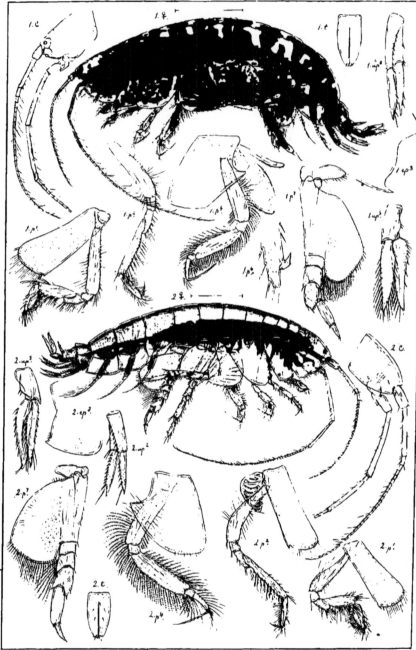

G.O.Sars autogr.

1. Ampelisca Eschrichtij, Kröyer.
2. Ampelisca odontoplax, G.O.Sars.

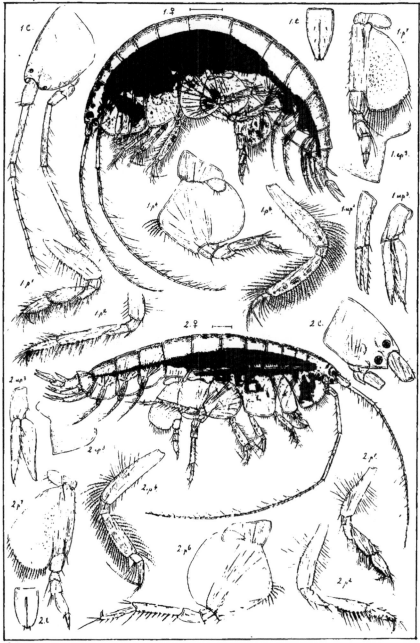

G.O.Sars autogr.

1. Ampelisca æqvicornis, Bruzelius.
2. Ampelisca anomala, G.O.Sars.

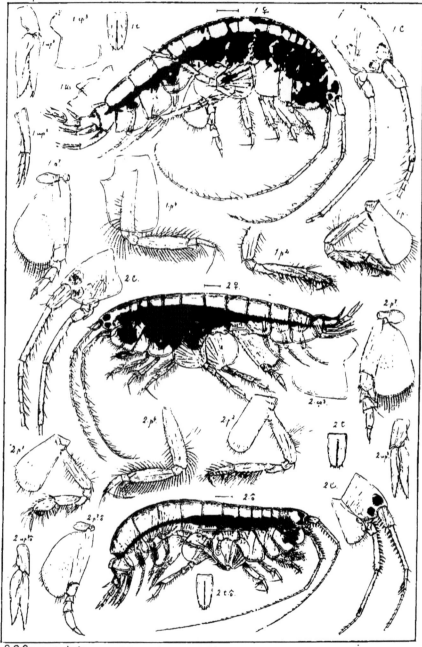

C.O.Sars autogr.   1.Ampelisca. amblyops, n. sp.
2.Ampelisca pusilla, n. sp.

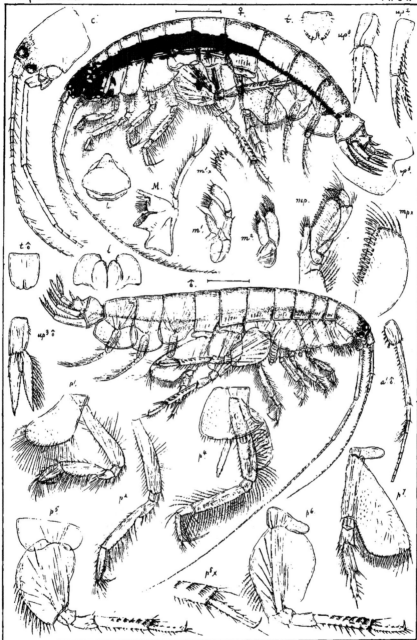

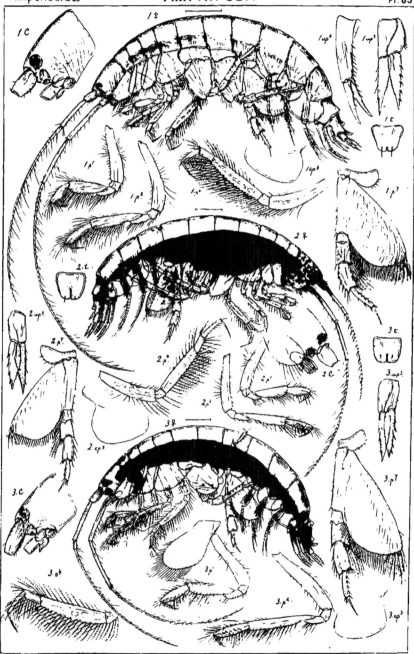

G O Sars autogr.

1. Byblis longicornis, n. sp.
2 Byblis affinis, n. sp.
3 Byblis erythrops, G.O.Sars.

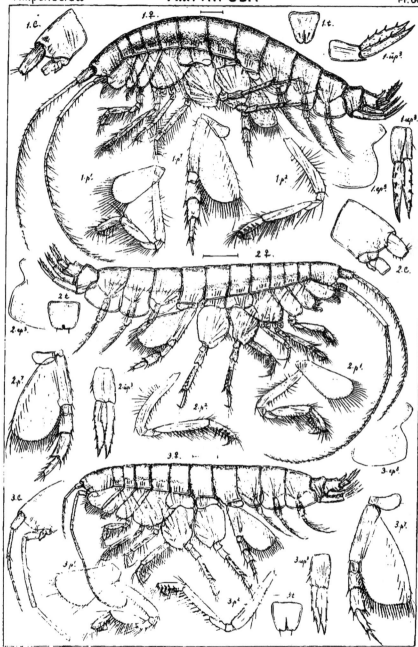

1. Byblis crassicornis, Metzger
2. Byblis abyssi, G.O.Sars.
3. Byblis minuticornis, G.O.Sars.

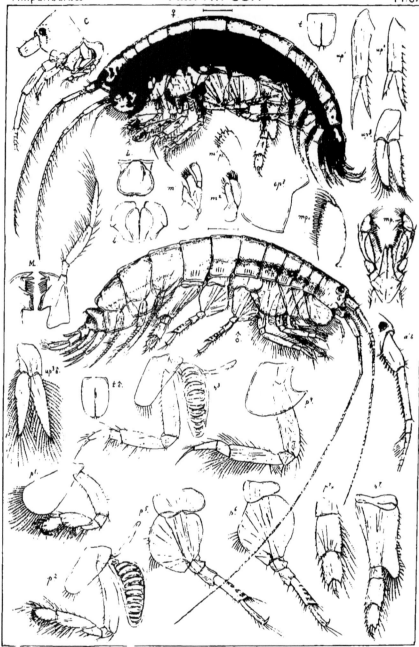

G.O.Sars autogr.   Haploops tubicola, Lilljeborg.

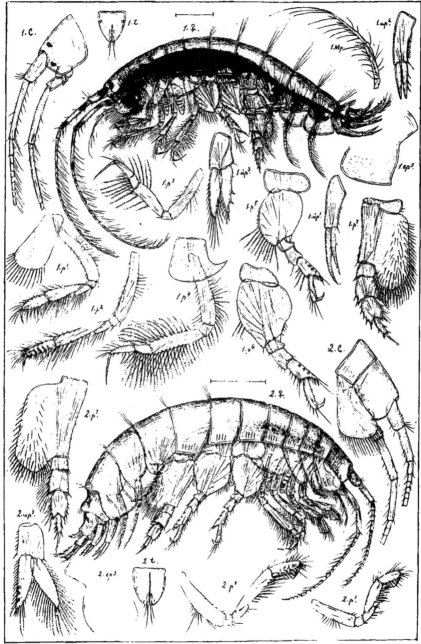

G.O.Sars autogr.

1. Haploops setosa, Boeck
2. Haploops robusta, n.sp.

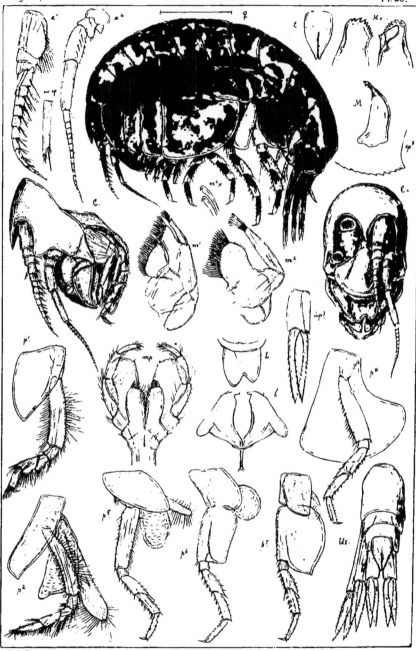

G.O.Sars autogr. Stegocephalus inflatus, Kröyer.

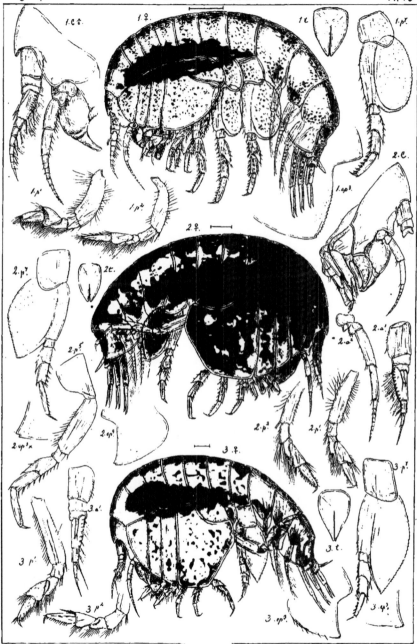

G.O Sars autogr.

1. Stegocephalus similis, n. sp.
2 Stegocephaloides christianiensis, Boeck.
3 Stegocephaloides auratus, G.O.Sars.

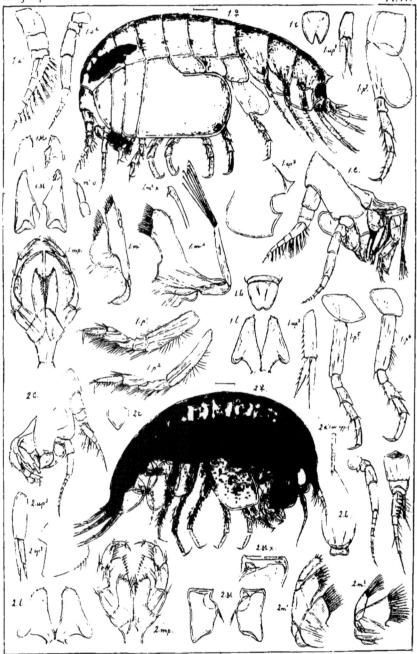

1. Aspidopleurus gibbosus, G.O.Sars.
                                         2. Andania abyssi, Boeck.

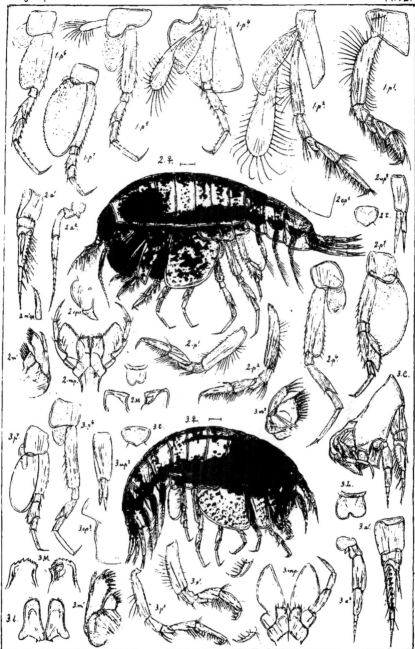

G.O.Sars autogr.

1. Andania abyssi, Boeck.
2. Andaniopsis nordlandica, (Boeck.)
3. Andaniella pectinata, G.O.Sars.

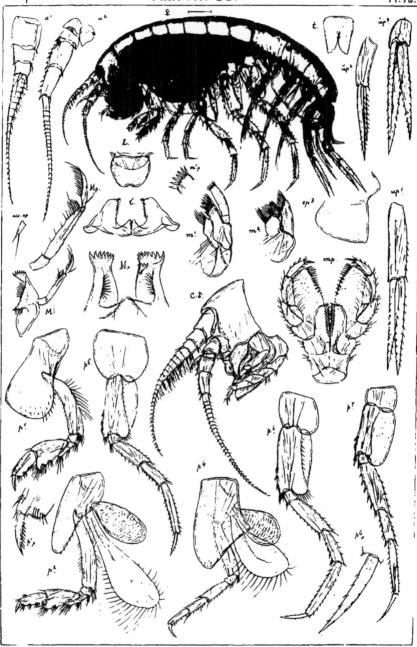

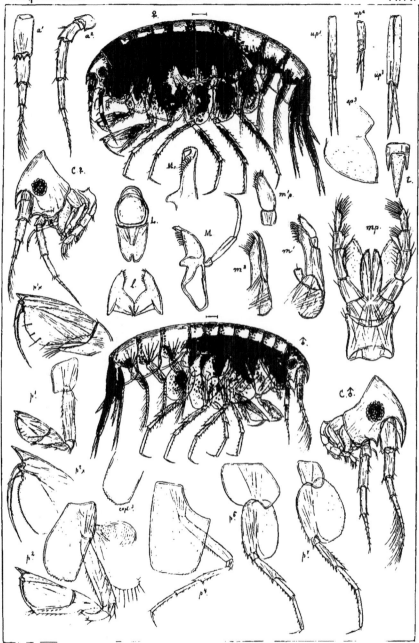

Amphilochus manudens, Sp. Bate.

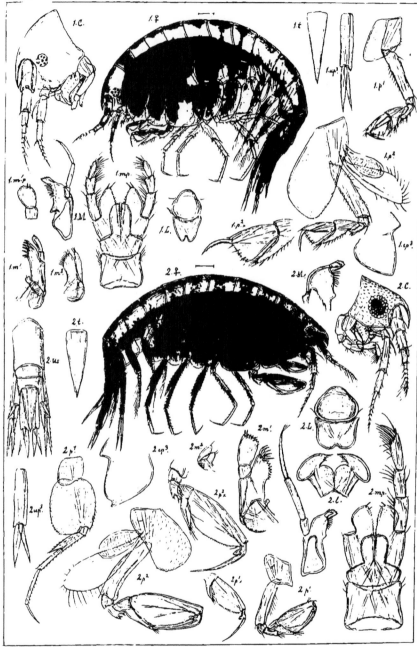

1. Amphilochus tenuimanus, Boeck.
2. Amphilochoides odontonyx (Boeck).

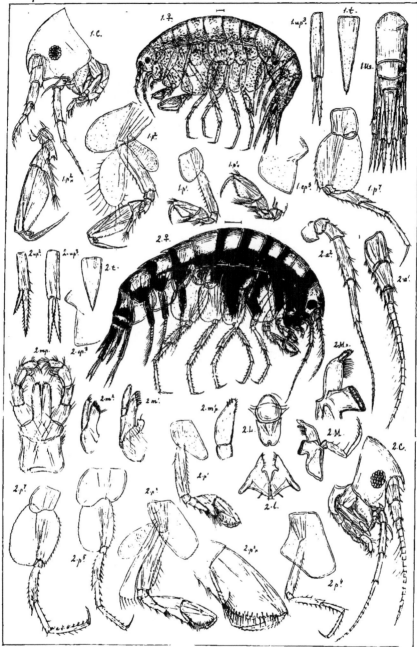

G.O.Sars autogr

1. Amphilochoides pusillus, n. sp.
2. Gitanopsis bispinosa, (Boeck).

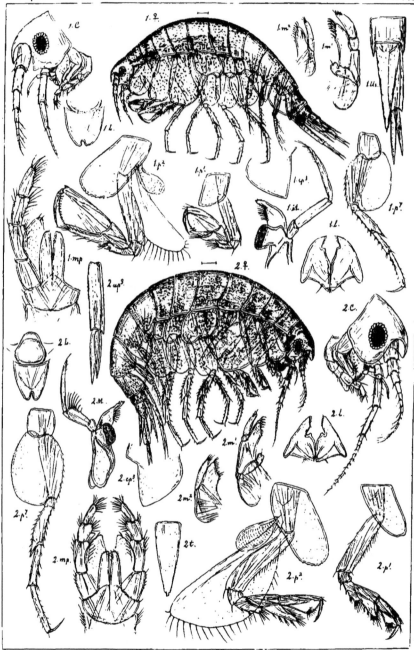

G.O.Sars autogr.

1. Gitanopsis inermis, G.O.Sars
2. Gitanopsis arctica, n.sp.

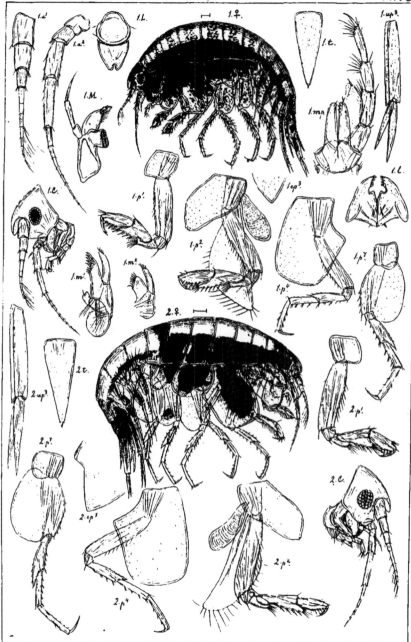

G.O.Sars autogr.

1. Gitana Sarsii, Boeck
2. Gitana abyssicola, n.sp.

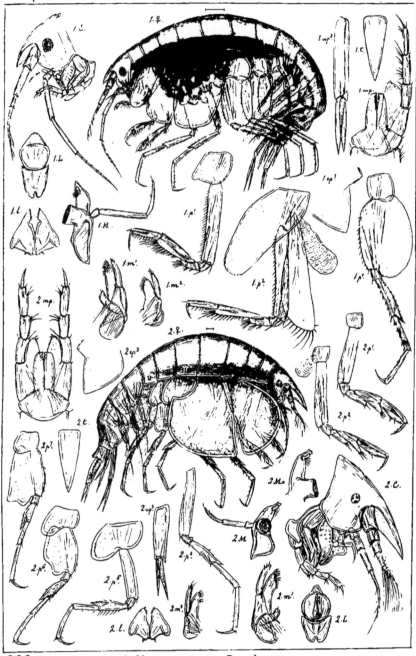

1. Gitana rostrata, Boeck
2 Stegoplax longirostris, G.O.Sars

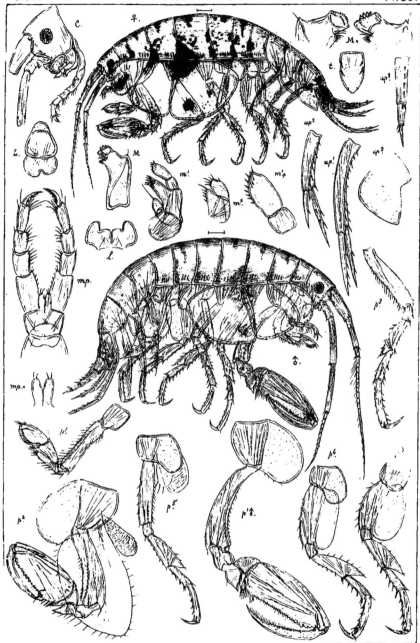

G.O Sars autogr.　　Stenothoe marina, (Sp. Bate).

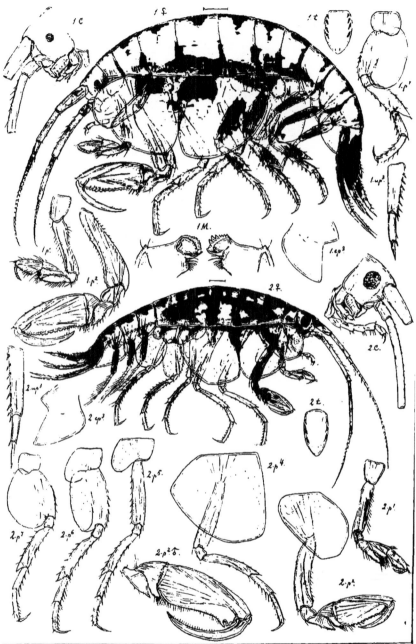

G.O.Sars autogr.

1. Stenothoe microps, n.sp.
2. Stenothoe tenella, G.O.Sars.

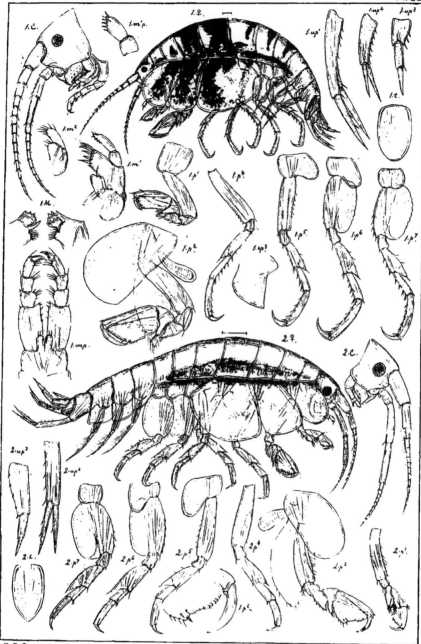

1. Stenothoe monoculoides, (Sp. Bate)
2. Stenothoe   brevicornis, G.O. Sars.

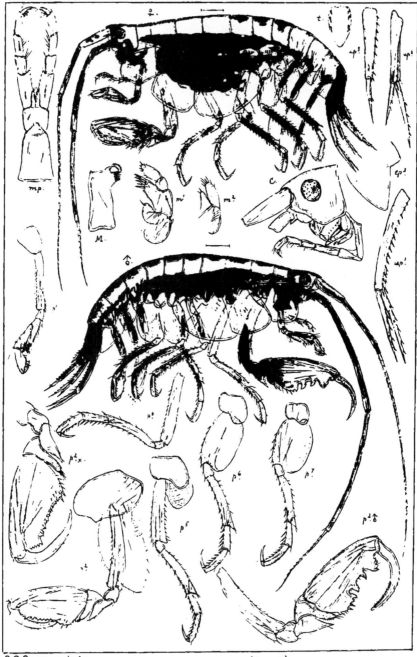

G O Sars autogr.   Stenothoe megacheir, (Boeck).

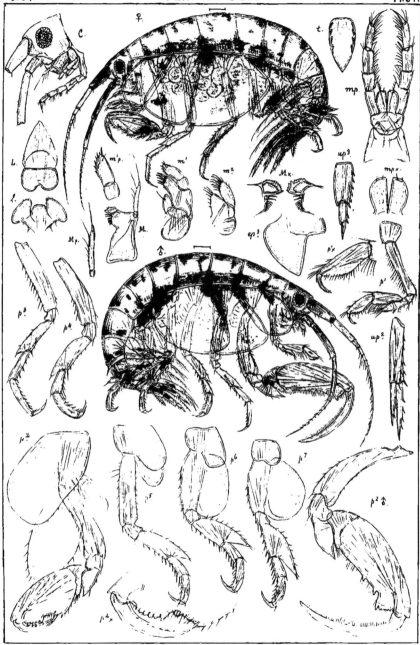

G.O.Sars autogr. Probolium gregarium, G.O.Sars

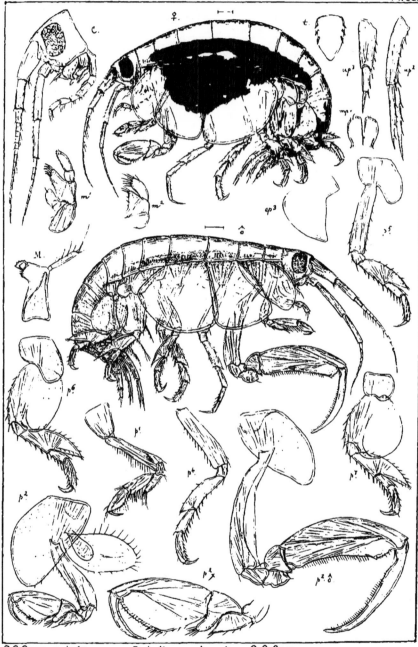

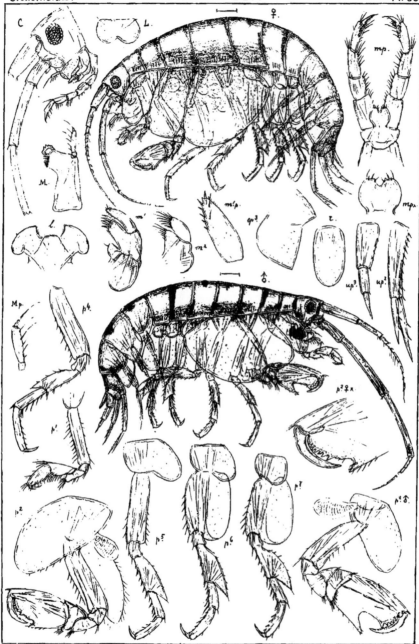

Metopa Alderi, (Sp. Bate)

Metopa spectabilis, G.O.Sars

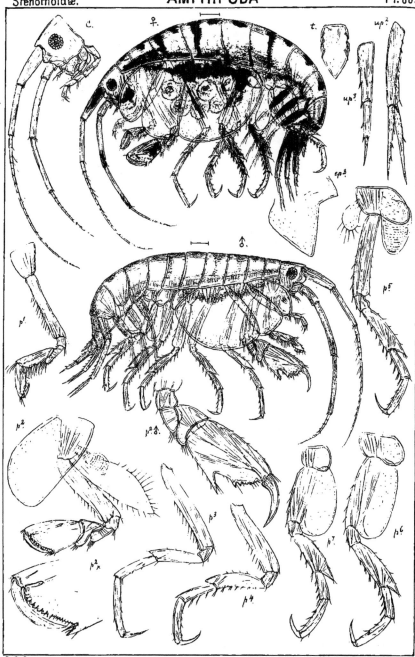

Metopa Boeckii, n.sp.

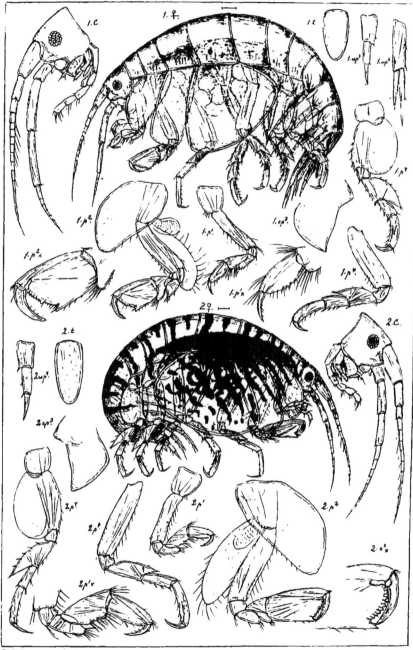

1. Metopa borealis, G.O. Sars.
2. Metopa rubrovittata, G.O. Sars.

G.O.Sars autogr

1. Metopa pusilla, n.sp.
2. Metopa longicornis, Boeck.

1. Metopa tenuimana, n. sp.
2. Metopa affinis, Boeck.

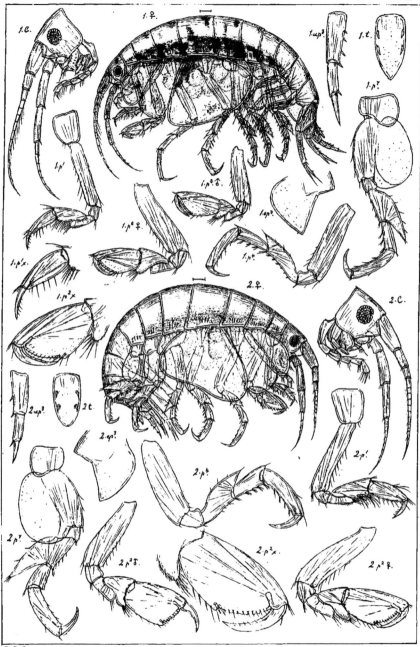

G.O.Sars autogr.　1. Metopa Bruzelii, Goës.
　　　　　　　　　2. Metopa sinuata, n. sp.

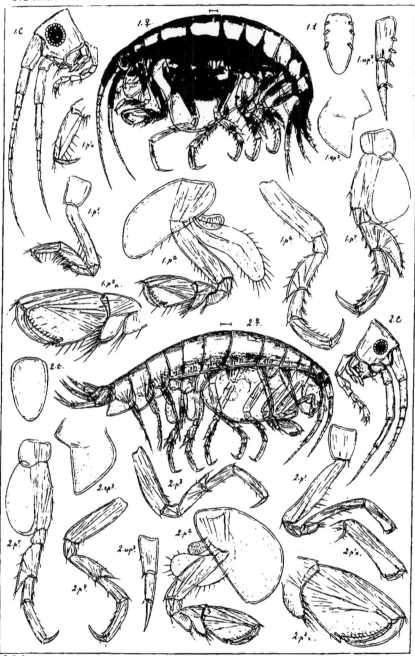

G.O.Sars autogr.

1. Metopa propinqva, n. sp.
2. Metopa leptocarpa, G.O.Sars.

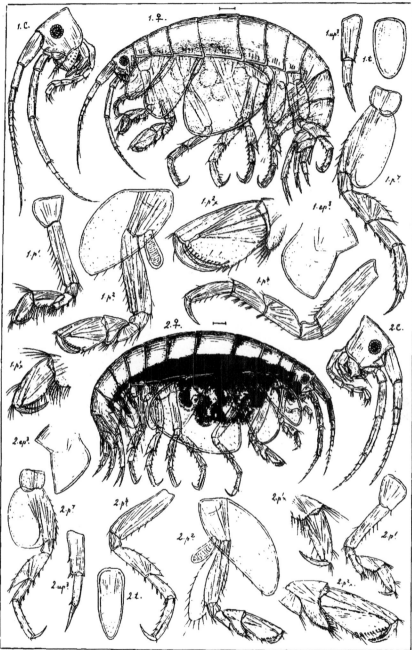

G.O.Sars autogr. 1. Metopa Sölsbergi, Schneider.
2. Metopa invalida, n. sp.

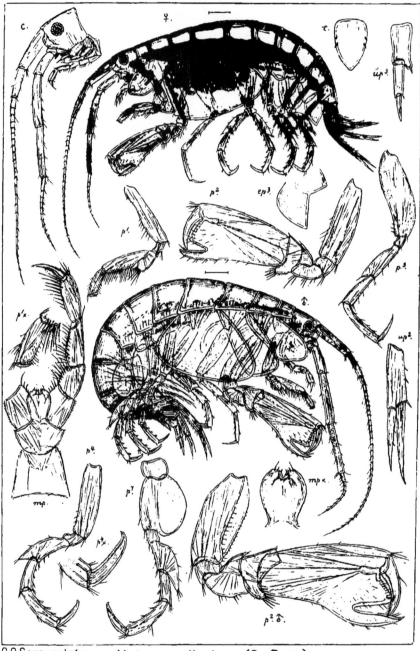

G.O.Sars autogr.   Metopa pollexiana,(Sp.Bate.)

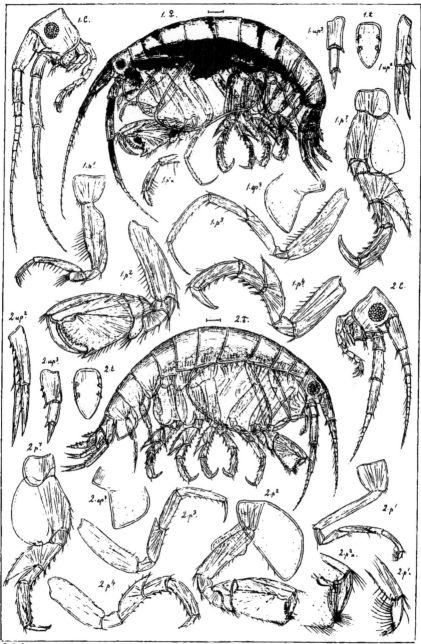

G O Sars autogr.

1. Metopa robusta, n.sp.
2. Metopa palmata, n.sp.

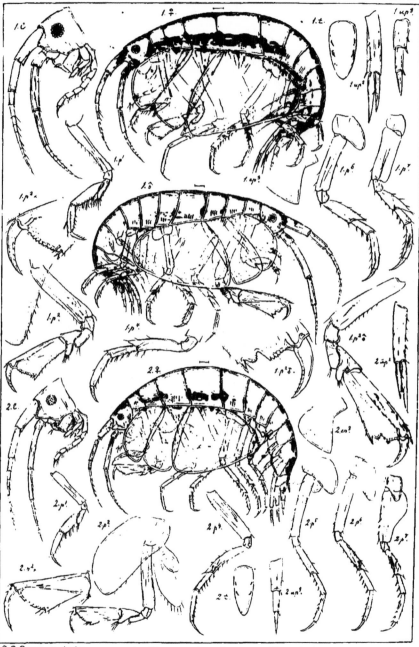

1. Metopa longimana, Boeck.
2. Metopa neglecta, Hansen.

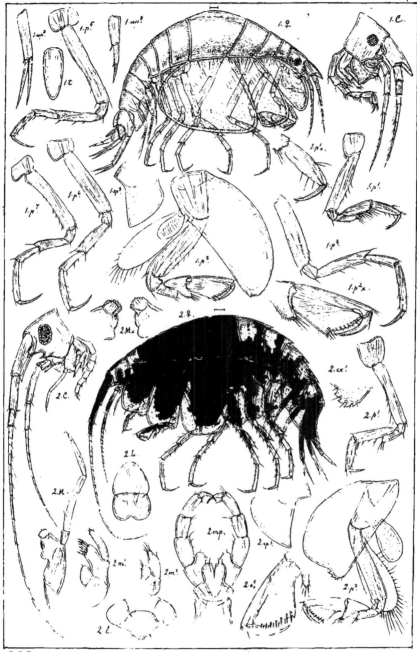

1. Metopa nasuta, Boeck.
2. Cressa dubia, (Sp. Bate).

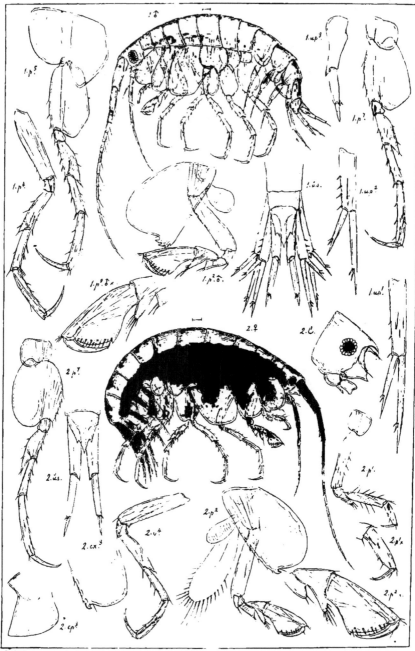

G.O.Sars autogr.

1. Cressa dubia, (Sp. Bate).
2. Cressa minuta, Boeck.

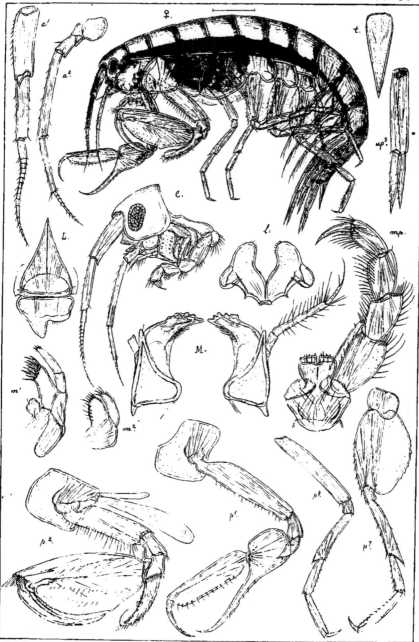

G.O.Sars autogr   Leucothoe articulosa, Abildg.

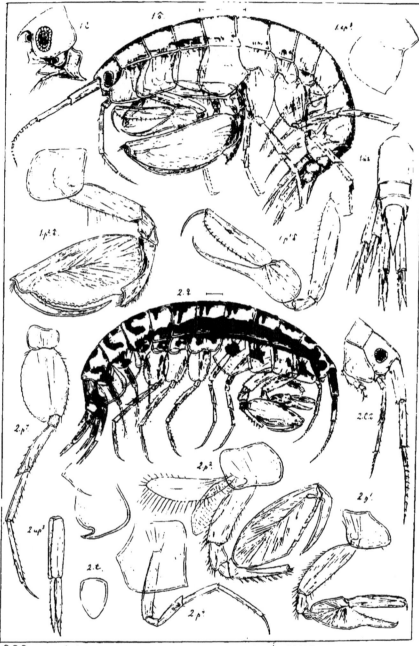

G O Sars autogr.

1. Leucothoe articulosa, Abildg. ♂
2. Leucothoe imparicornis, Norm.

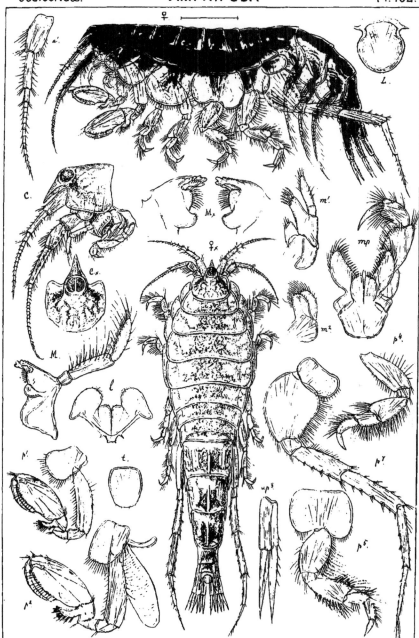

Oediceros saginatus, Kröyer.

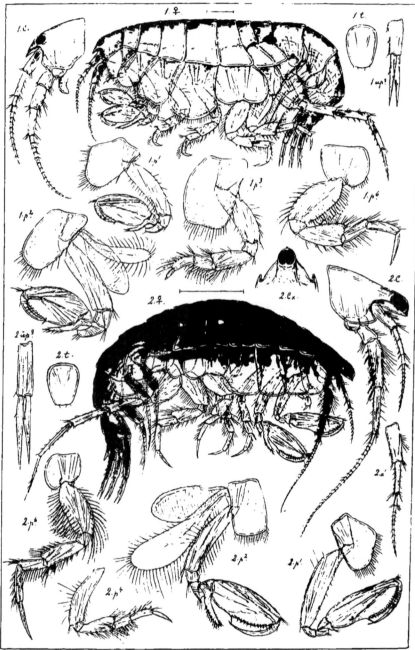

G O Sars autogr.

1. Oediceros borealis, Boeck.
2. Paroediceros lynceus, (M. Sars).

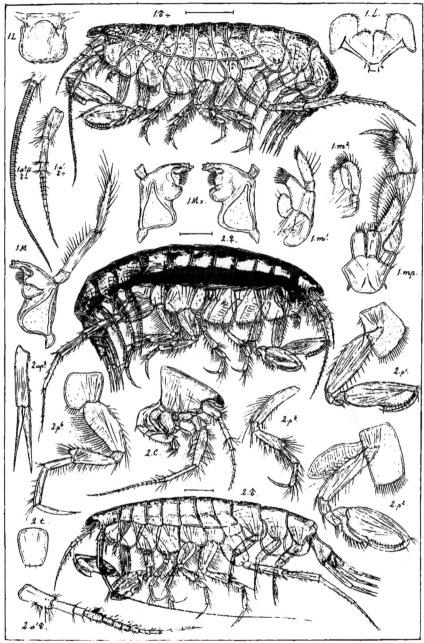

1. Paroediceros lynceus, (M. Sars).
2. Paroediceros propinqvus, (Goës).

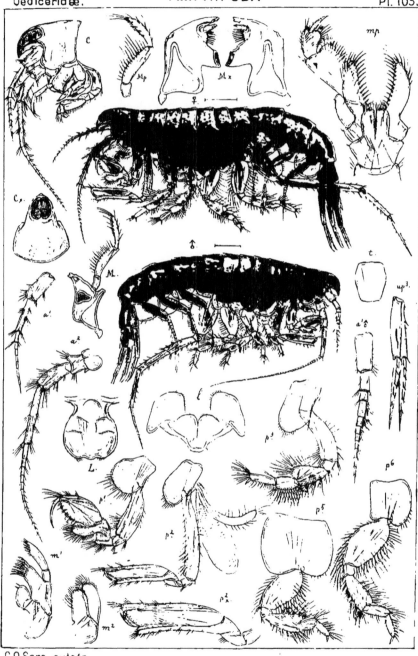

G.O.Sars autogr.

Monoculodes carinatus, Sp. Bate

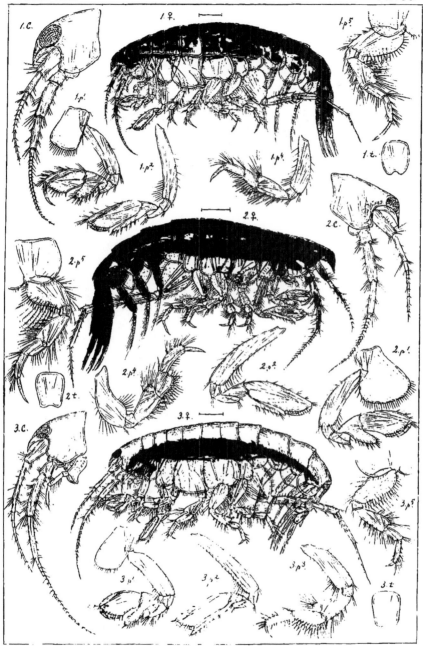

C.O.Sars autogr.   1.Monoculodes tessellatus, Schneider.
2.Monoculodes borealis, Bœck.
3.Monoculodes pallidus, n.sp.

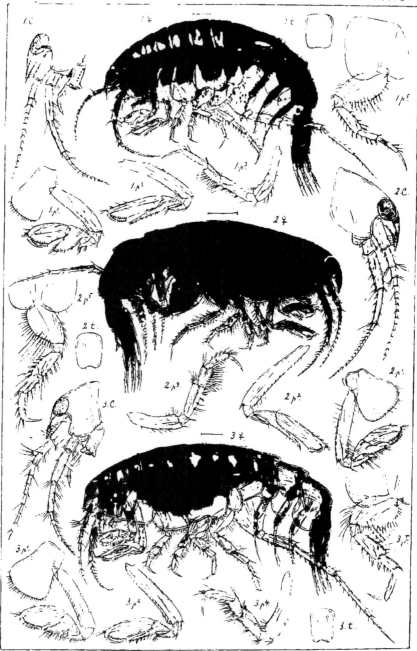

1. Monoculodes norvegicus, Boeck.
2. Monoculodes falcatus, n. sp.
3. Monoculodes tuberculatus, Boeck.

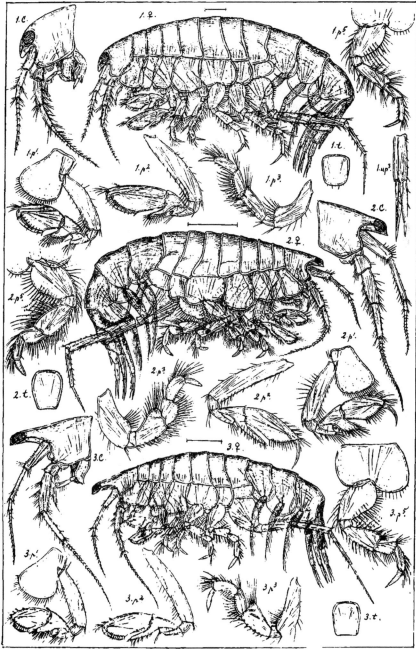

G.O.Sars autogr.

1. Monoculodes latimanus, (Goës.)
2. Monoculodes Kröyeri, Boeck.
3. Monoculodes longirostris, (Goës.)

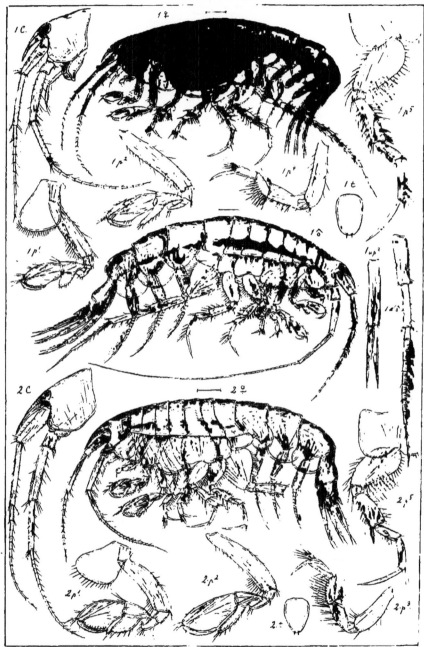

G.O Sars autogr.   1. Monoculodes Packardi, Boeck.
2. Monoculodes tenuirostratus, Boeck.

1. Monoculopsis longicornis (Boeck)
2. Perioculodes longimanus, (Sp. Bate.)

G.O.Sars autogr

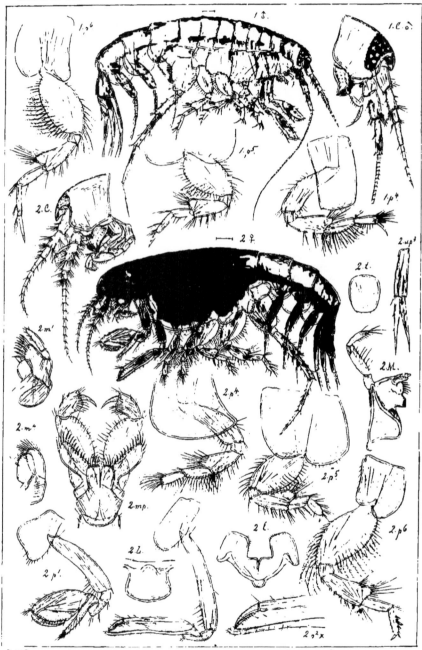

G.U.Sars autogr.   1. Perioculodes longimanus, (Sp.Bate.)
2 Pontocrates norvegicus, Boeck.

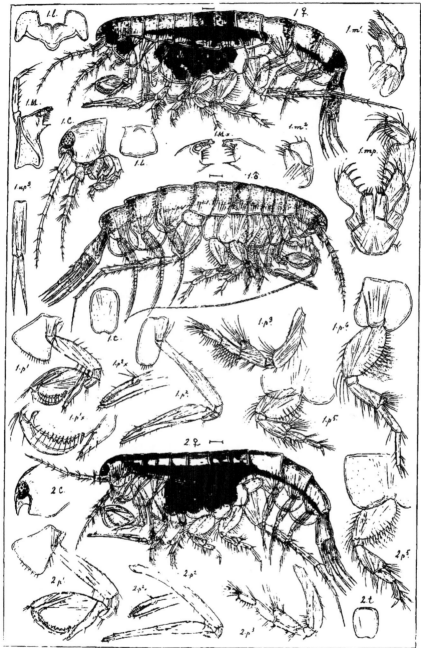

G.O.Sars autogr.

1. Synchelidium brevicarpum, (Sp. Bate).
2. Synchelidium haplocheles, (Grube).

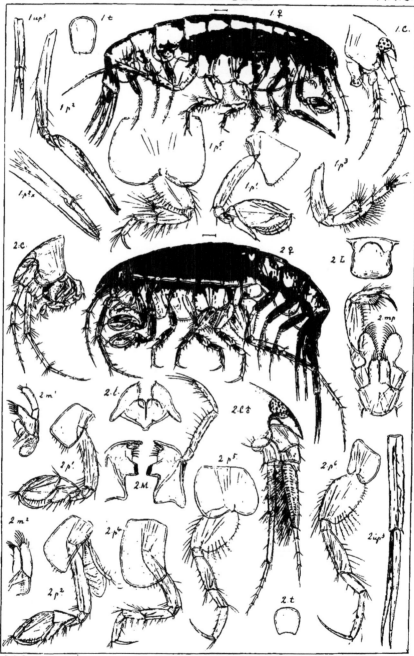

G.O.Sars autogr.

1. Synchelidium intermedium, n.sp.
2. Halicreion longicaudatus, Boeck.

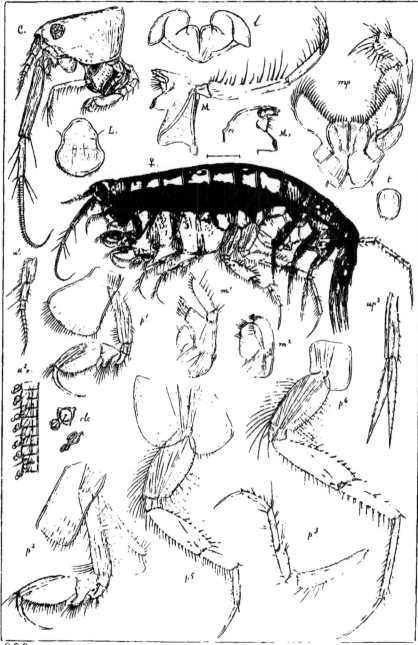

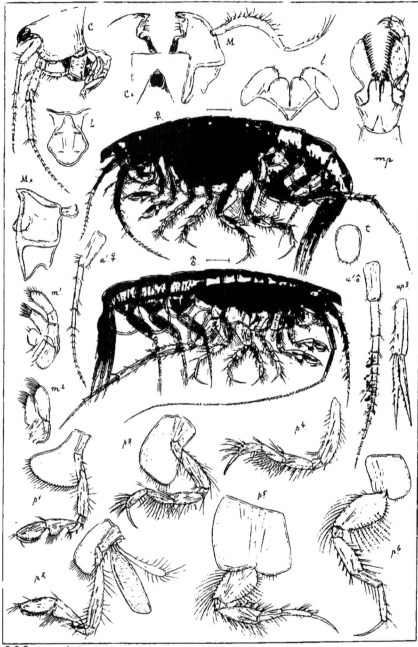

Halimedon Mülleri, Boeck.

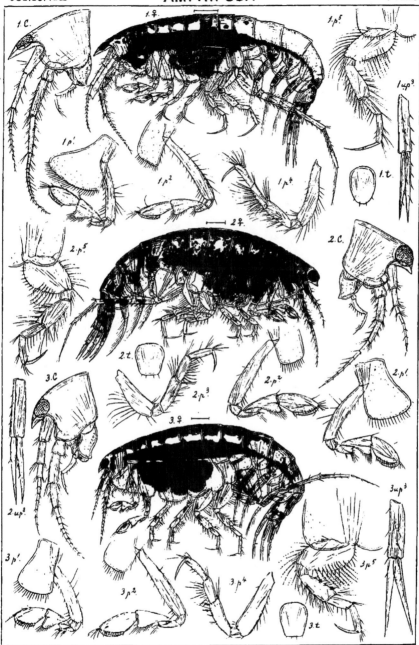

G O Sars autogr.

1. Halimedon acutifrons, n, sp.
2. Halimedon megalops, G.O.Sars.
3. Halimedon brevicalcar, (Goës).

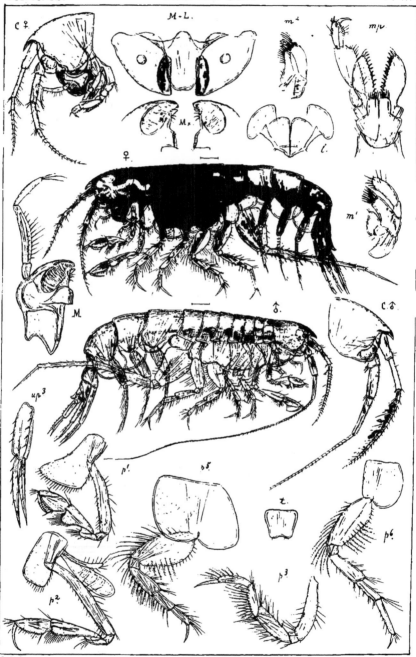

G.O.Sars autogr   Bathymedon longimanus, (Boeck).

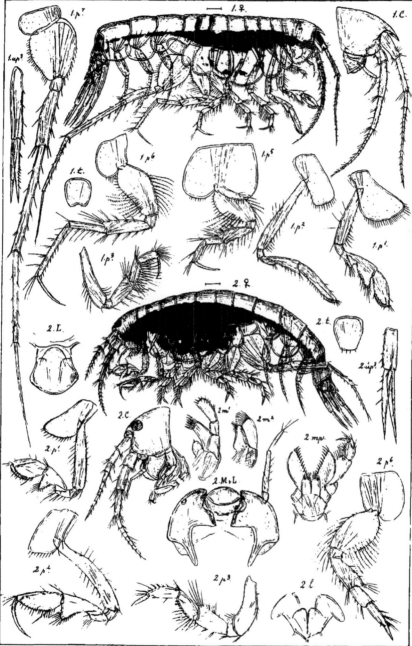

1. Bathymedon Saussurei, (Boeck).
2. Bathymedon obtusifrons, (Hansen).

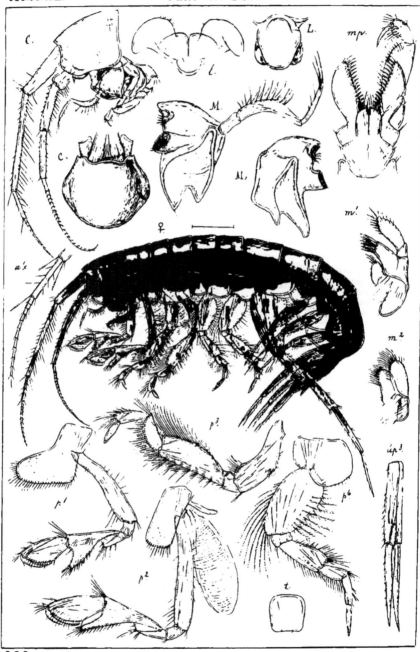

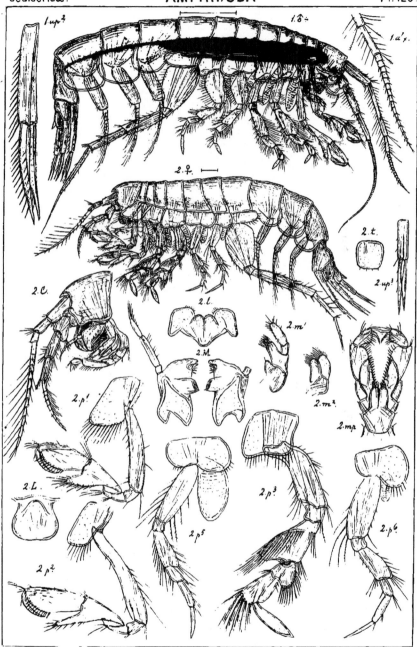

G.O.Sars autogr.

1. Aceros phyllonyx, (M.Sars).
2. Aceropsis latipes, G.O.Sars.

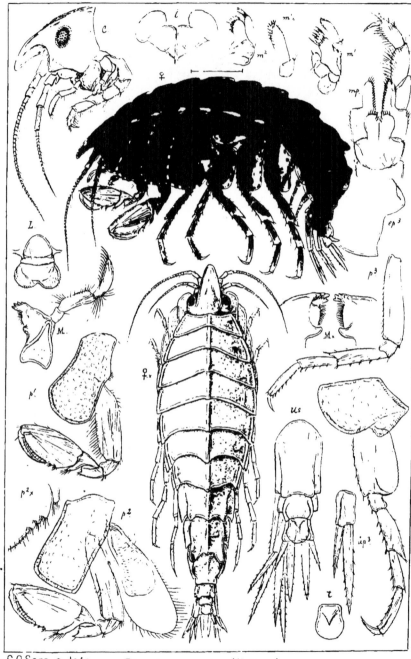

G.O.Sars autogr. Pleustes panoplus, (Kröyer.)

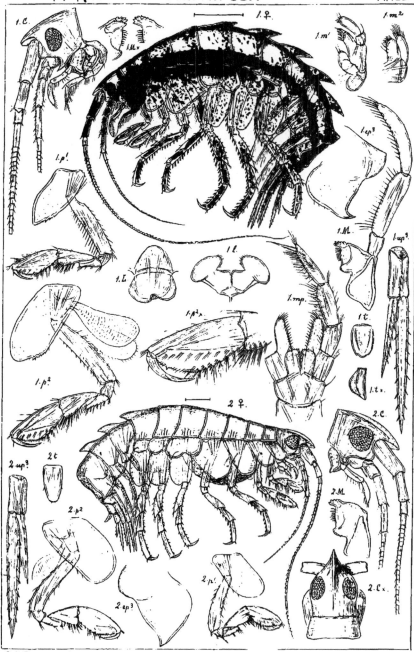

GOSars autogr.

1. Paramphithoë pulchella, (Kröyer).
2. Paramphithoë Boeckü, Hansen.

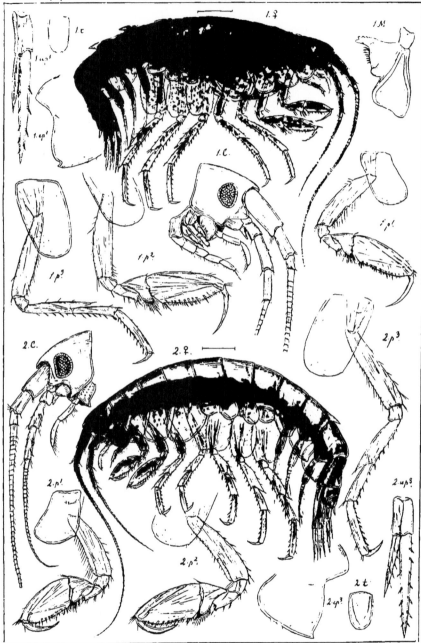

G.O.Sars autogr.   1. Paramphithoë bicuspis, (Kröyer).
2 Paramphithoë monocuspis, n.sp.

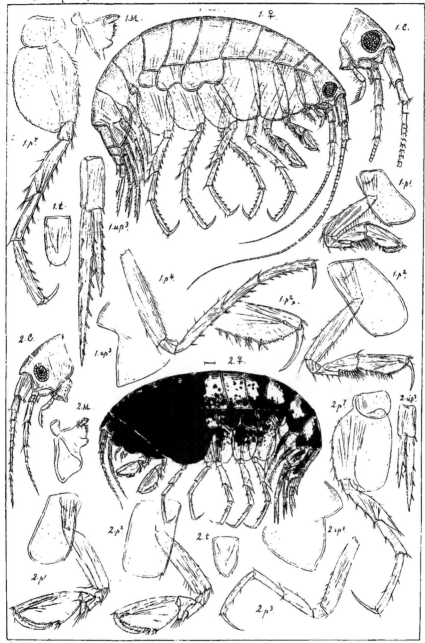

C O Sars autogr.   1. Paramphithoë assimilis, G.O.Sars.
2. Paramphilhoë brevicornis, G.O.Sars.

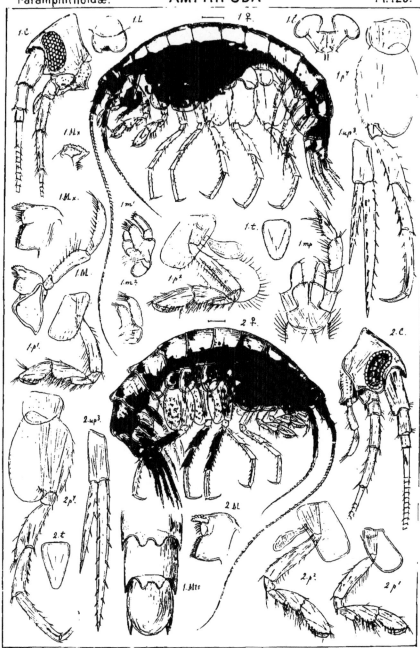

G.O.Sars autogr.

1.Stenopleustes Malmgreni, (Boeck).
2.Stenopleustes nodifer, G.O.Sars.

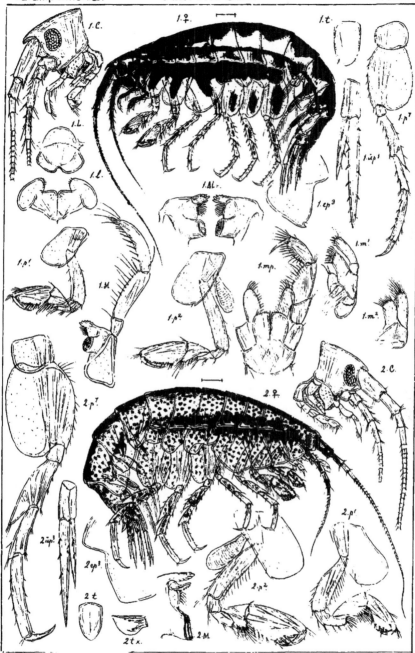

G.O.Sars autogr.

1.Parapleustes glaber,(Boeck).
2.Parapleustes pulchellus, G.O.Sars.

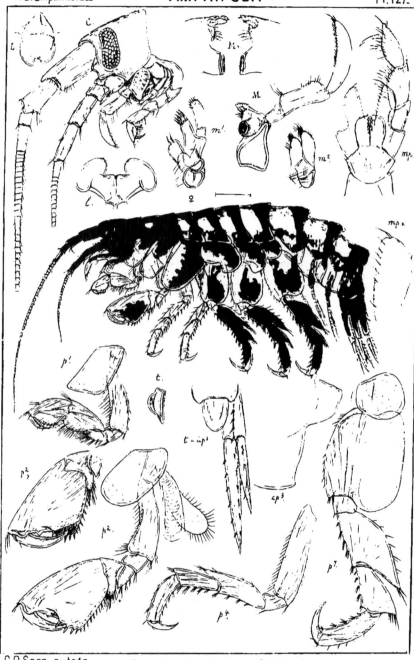

G.O.Sars autogr   Parapleustes latipes, (M.Sars).

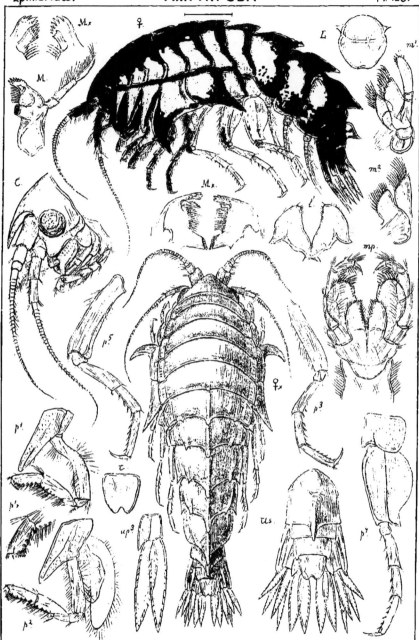

G.O.Sars autogr.　　　Epimeria cornigera, (Fabr.).

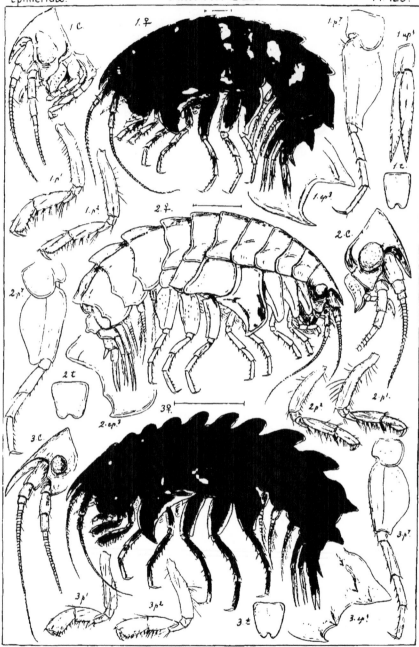

1. Epimeria parasitica, (M. Sars.)
2. Epimeria tuberculata. n. sp.
3 Epimeria loricata, G. O. Sars.

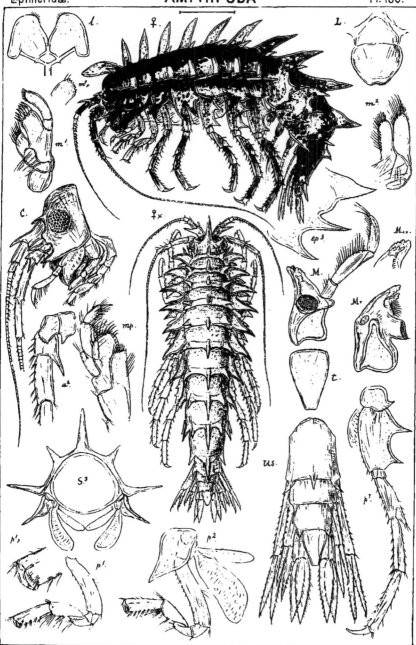

G.O.Sars autogr Acanthozone cuspidata, (Lepechin.)

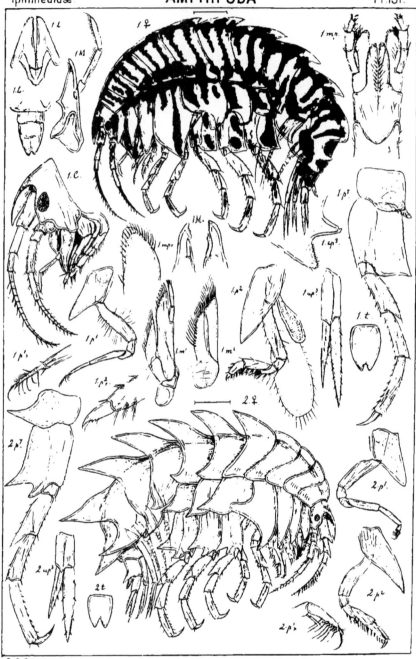

G.O.Sars autogr.   1.Acanthonotosoma serratum, (Fabr.)
2.Acanthonotosoma cristatum, (Owen.)

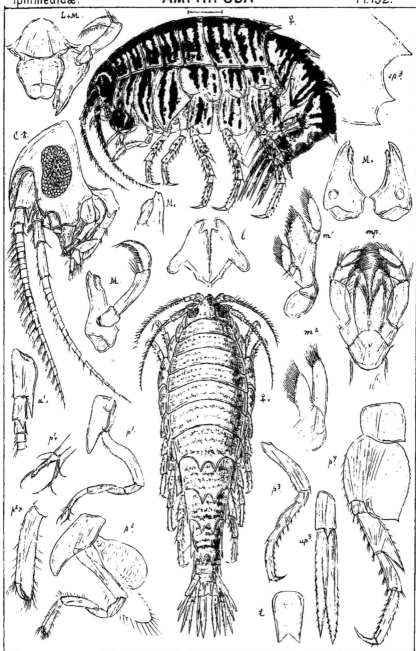

Iphimedia obesa, Rathke.

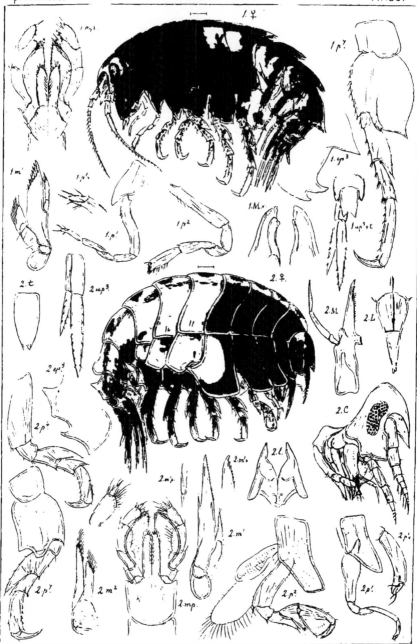

1. Iphimedia minuta, G. O. Sars.
2. Odius carinatus, (Sp. Bate.)

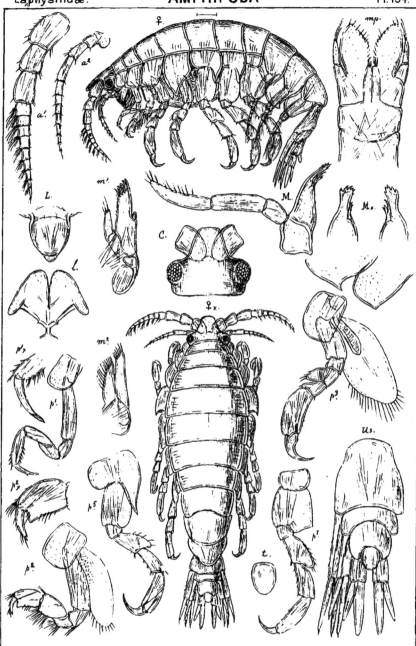

Laphystius sturionis, Kröyer.

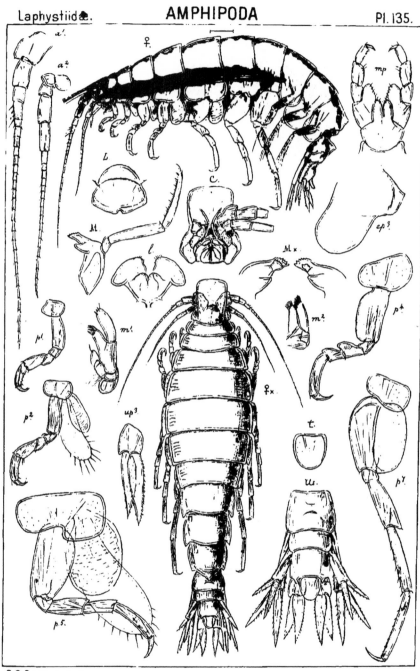

G.O.Sars autogr.   Laphystiopsis planifrons, n.gen. & sp.

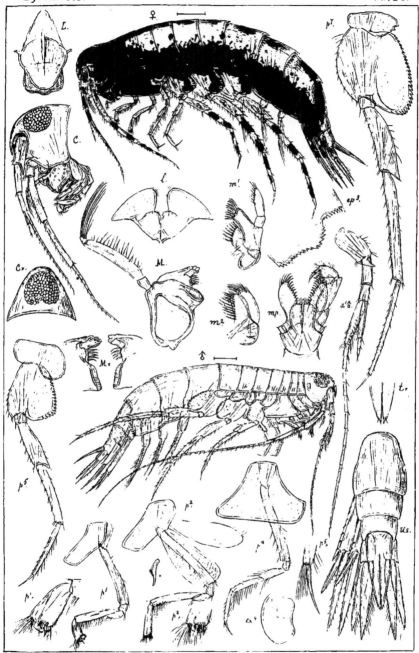

G.O.Sars autogr.　　Syrrhoë crenulata, Goës.

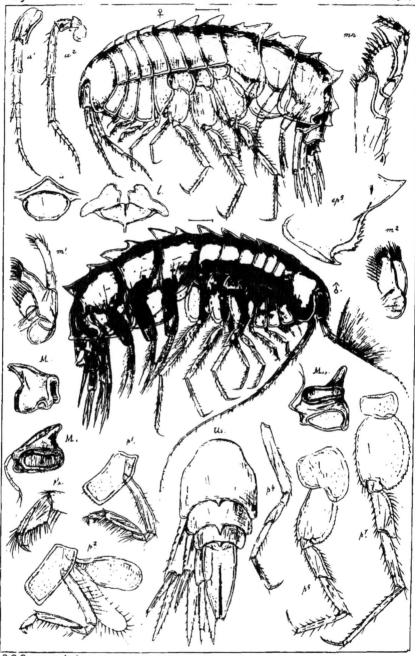

G O Sars autogr.   Syrrhoites serrata, G.O.Sars.

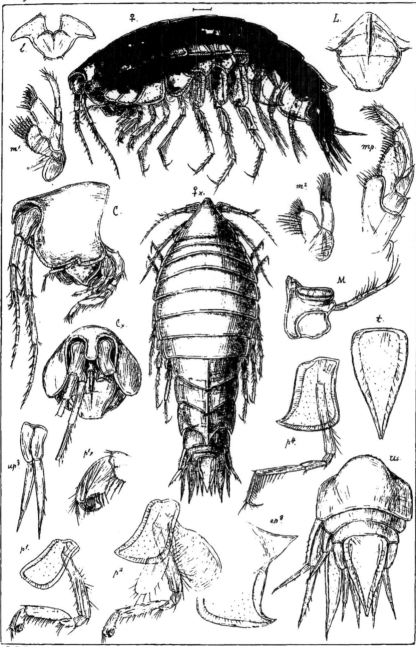

G.O.Sars autogr   Bruzelia typica, Boeck.

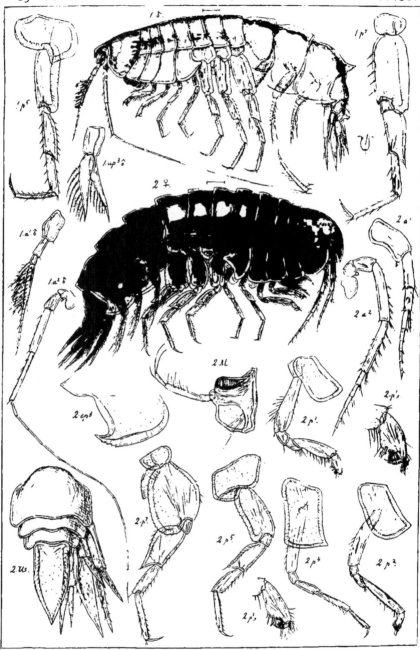

G.O.Sars autogr.

1. Bruzelia typica, Boeck.
2. Bruzelia tuberculata, G.O.Sars.

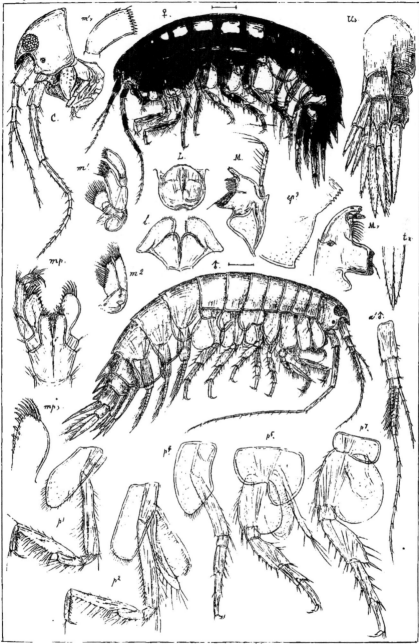

GO Sars autogr.

Tiron acanthurus, Lilljeborg.

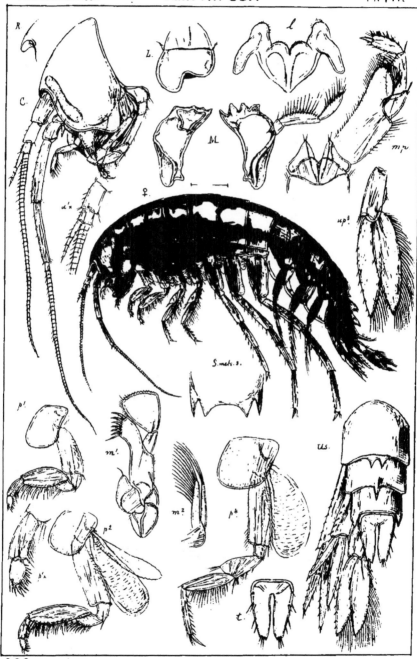

G.O.Sars autogr. Pardalisca cuspidata, Kröyer.

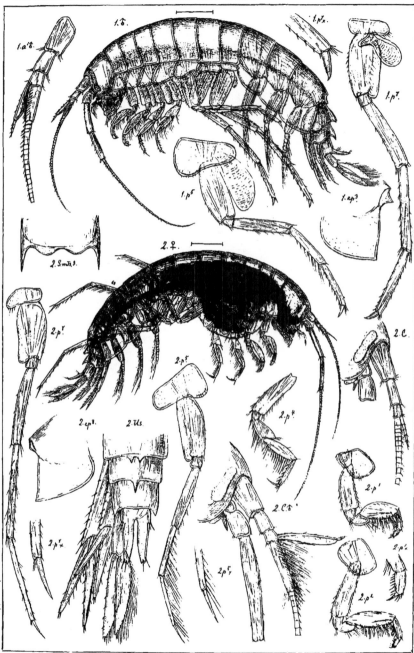

1. Pardalisca cuspidata, Kröyer.
2. Pardalisca tenuipes, n. sp.

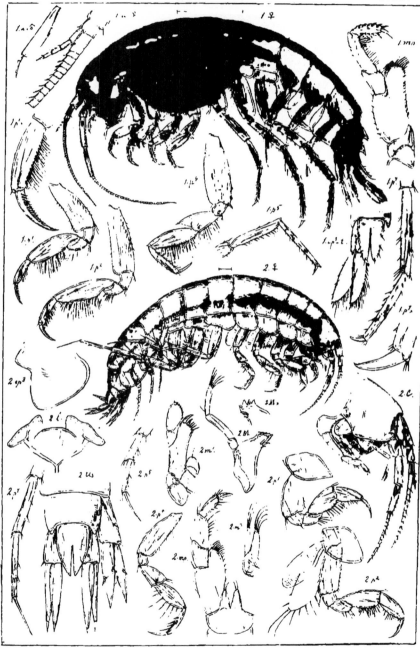

G.O.Sars autogr.   1. Pardalisca abyssi, Boeck.
                     2. Pardaliscella Boeckii,(Malm)

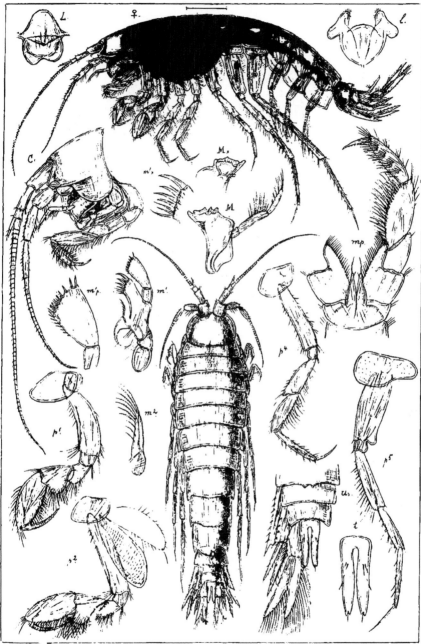

Nicippe tumida, Bruzelius.

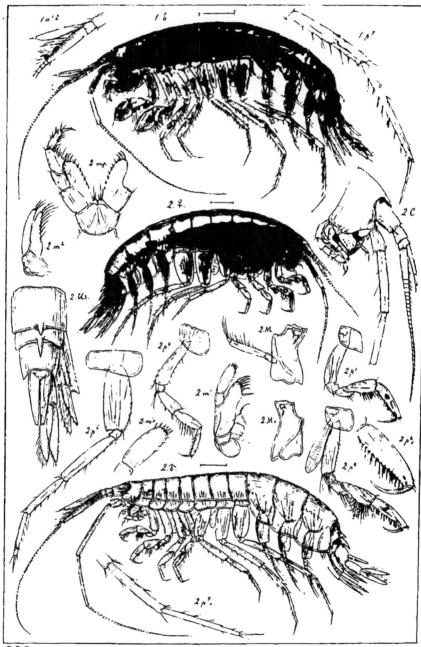

G.O.Sars autogr.

1. Nicippe tumida, Bruzel.
2. Halice abyssi, Boeck.

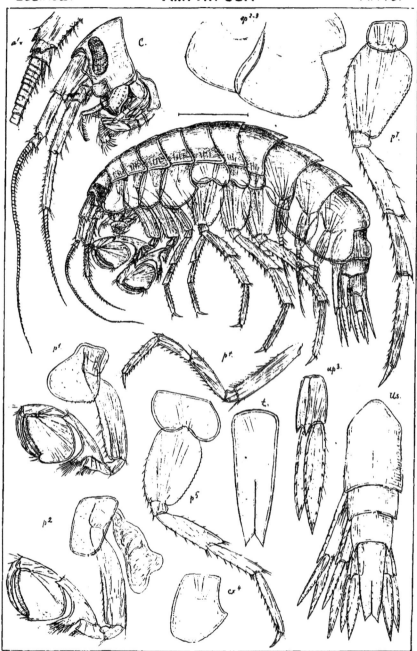

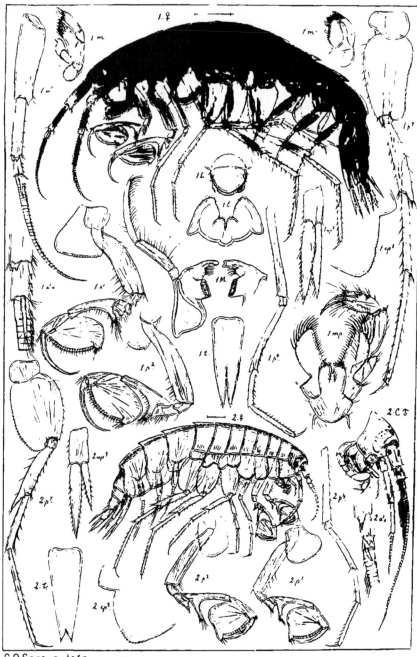

G.O.Sars autogr.   1. Eusirus propinqvus, n.sp.
2. Eusirus minutus, n.sp.

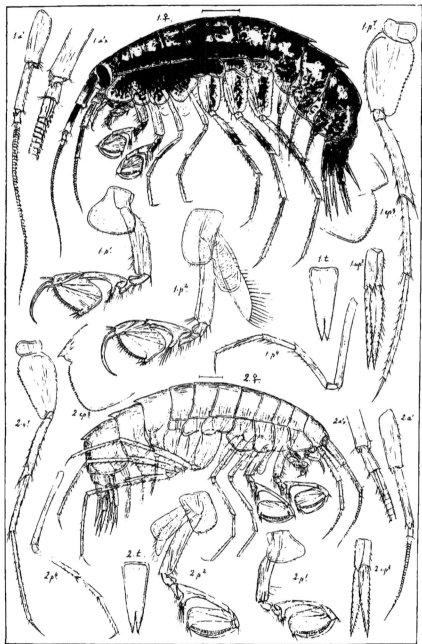

G.O.Sars autogr. 1. Eusirus longipes, Boeck.
2. Eusirus leptocarpus, n. sp.

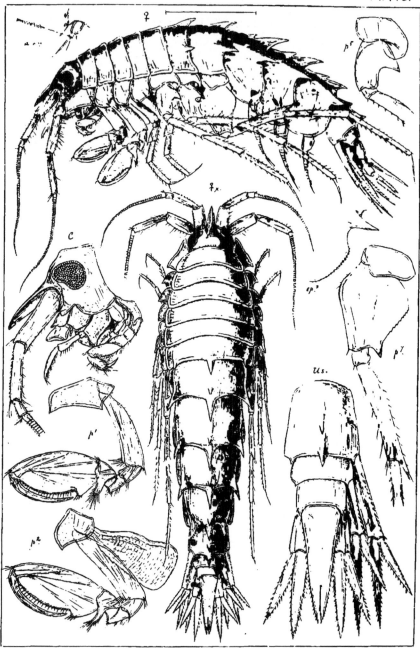

G.O.Sars autogr. Rhachotropis aculeata (Lepechin.)

G.O.Sars autogr.   Rhachotropis Helleri, (Boeck.)

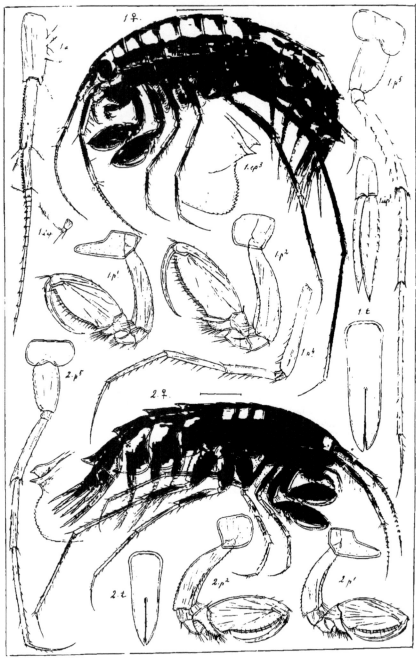

G.O Sars autogr.   1. Rhachotropis macropus, n.sp.
                     2. Rhachotropis leucophthalma, n.sp.

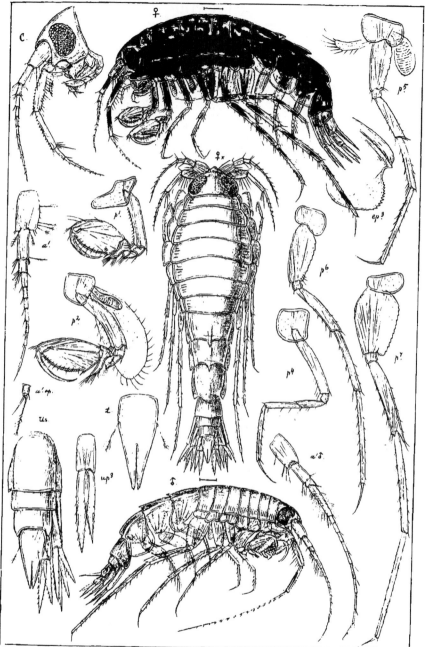

G.O.Sars autogr.   Rhachotropis tumida, G.O.Sars.

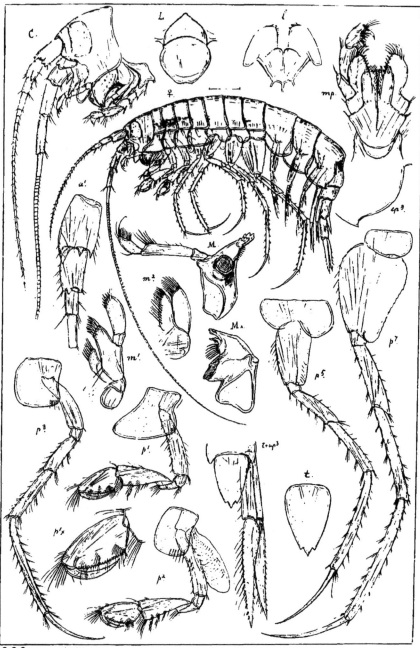

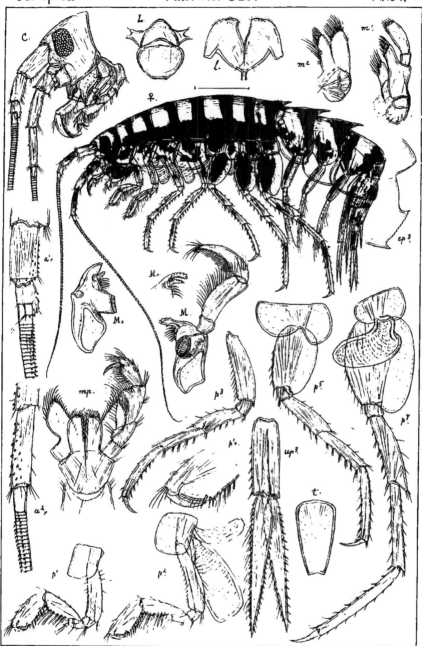

G.O.Sars autogr.   Halirages fulvocinctus, (M. Sars.)

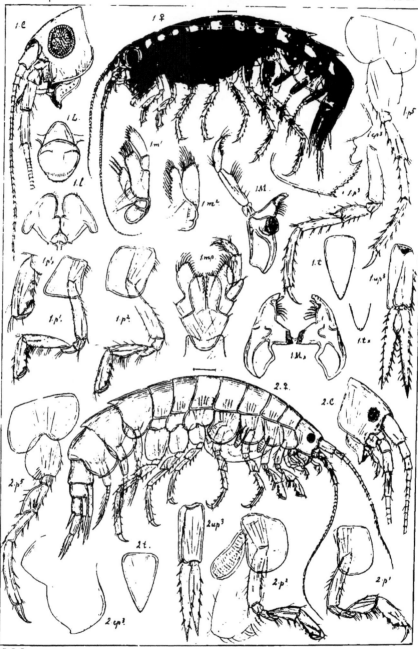

G.O.Sars autogr.   1. Apherusa bispinosa, (Sp. Bate.)
2. Apherusa borealis, (Boeck.)

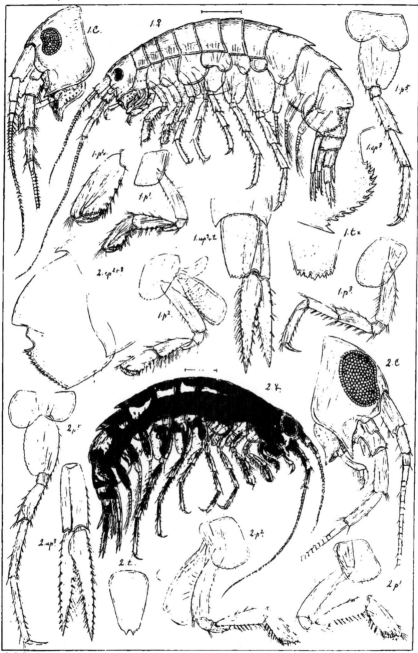

G.O.Sars autogr.

1. Apherusa tridentata. (Bruzel.)
2. Apherusa megalops. G.O.Sars.

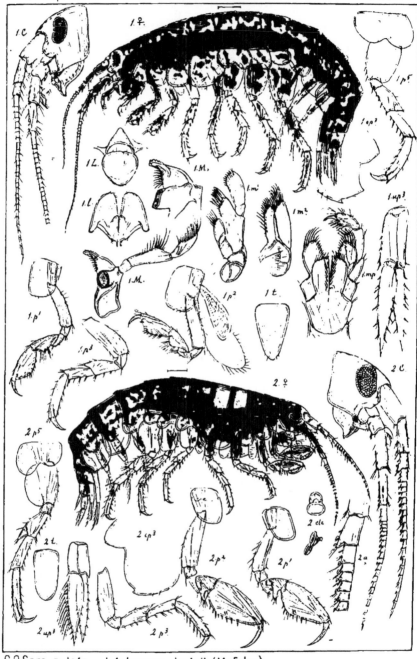

G.O.Sars autogr.   1. Apherusa Jurinii, (M-Edw.).
2. Calliopius Rathkei, (Zaddach.)

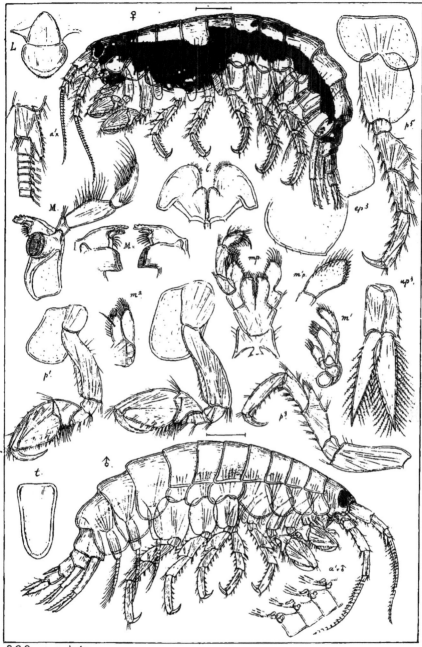

G.O.Sars autogr.   Calliopius læviusculus. (Kröyer.)

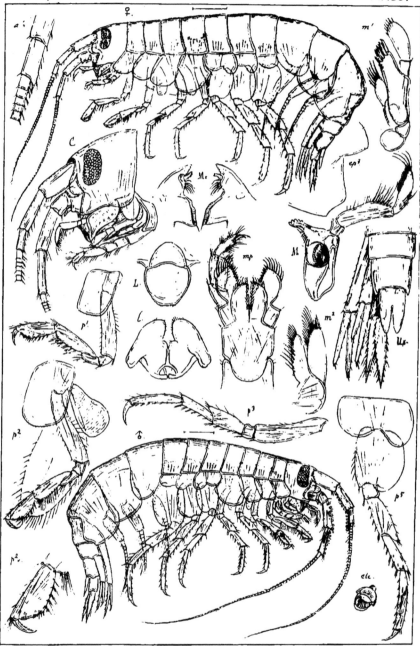

G.O Sars autogr.   Pontogeneia inermis, (Kröyer.)

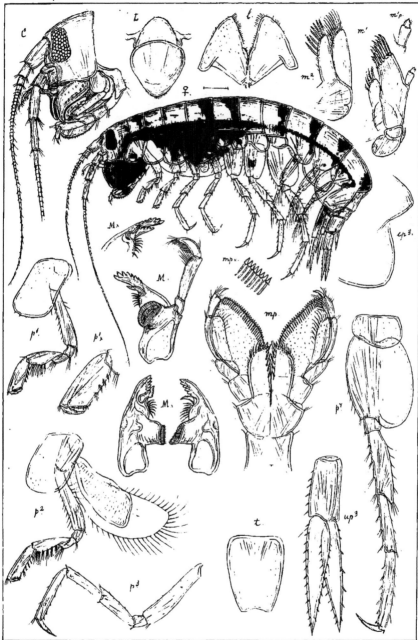

G.O.Sars autogr.   Laothoës Meinerti, Boeck.

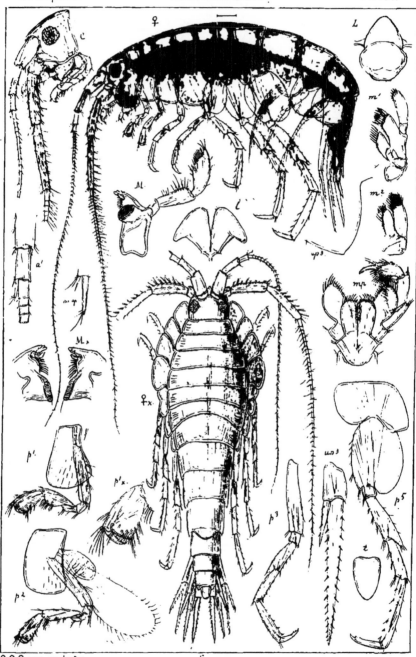

G.O.Sars autogr.   Amphithopsis longicaudata, Boeck.

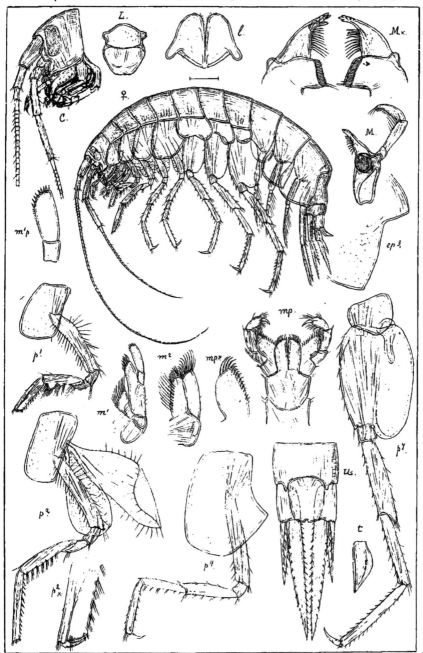

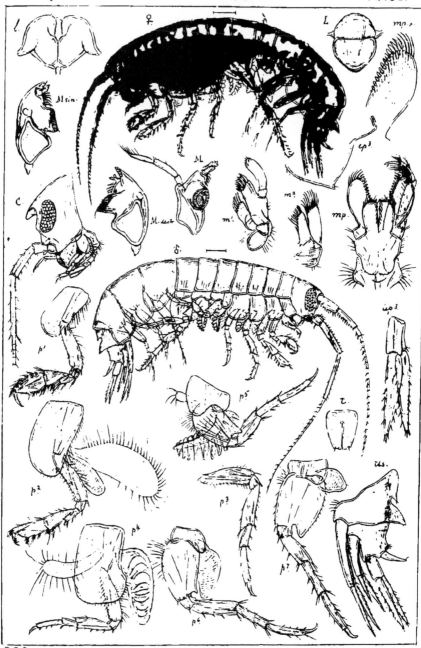

G O Sars autogr.

Paretylus· Swammerdami, (M-Edw.)

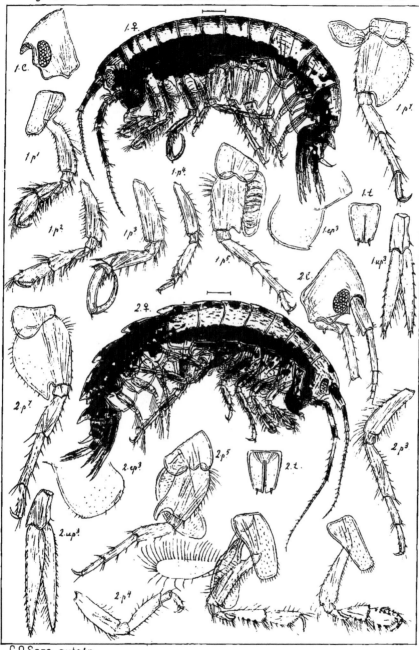

G.O.Sars autogr.

1. Paratylus falcatus, (Metzger.)
2. Paratylus vedlomensis, (Sp. Bate).

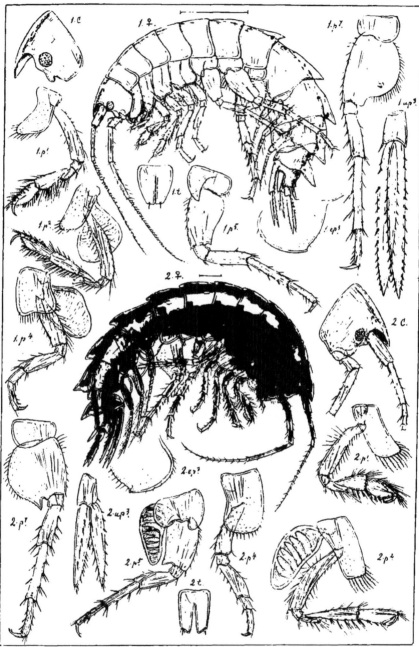

G.O.Sars autogr.   1. Paratylus Smithi, (Goës).
             2. Paratylus nordlandicus, (Boeck.)

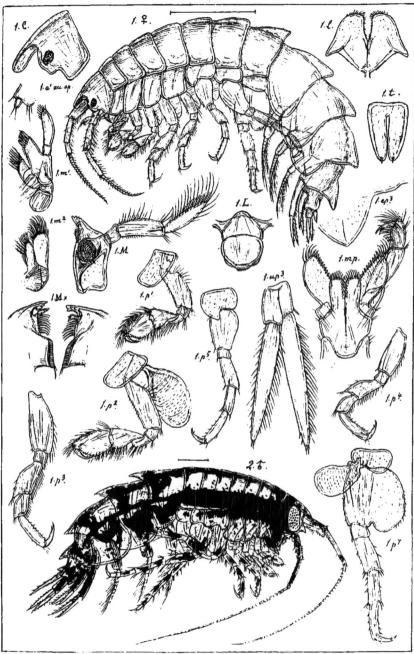

G.O.Sars autogr.

1. Atylus carinatus, (Fabr.)
2. Dexamine spinosa, (Mont.) ♂.

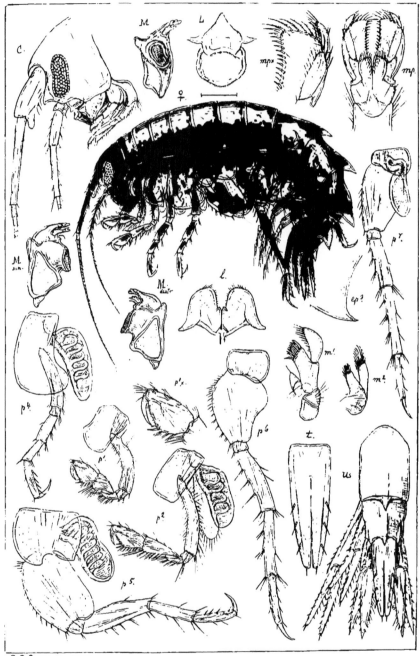

Dexamine spinosa, (Mont.) ♀.

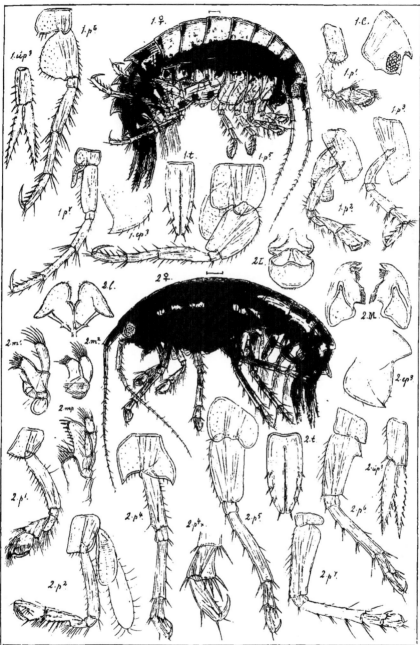

G.O.Sars autogr.

1 Dexamine Thea, Boeck.
2. Tritæta gibbosa, (Sp. Bate.)

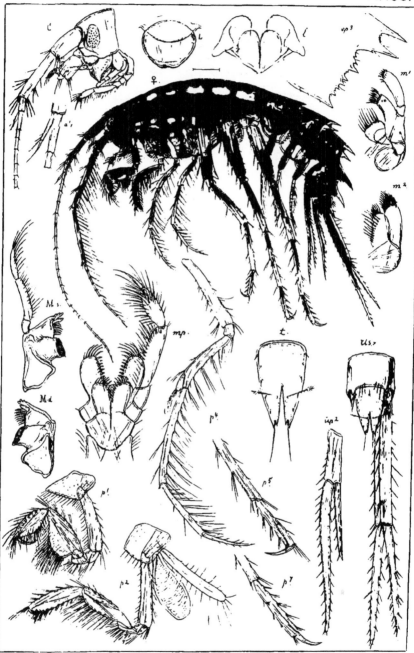

G O Sars autogr.

Melphidippa spinosa, (Goës.)

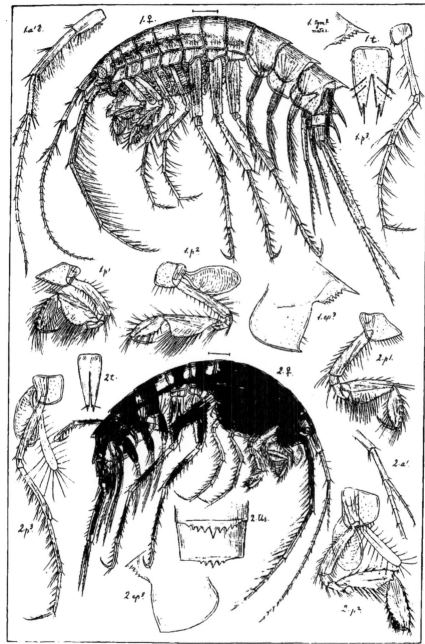

G O Sars autogr.

1. Melphidippa macrura, n.sp.
2. Melphidippa borealis, Boeck.

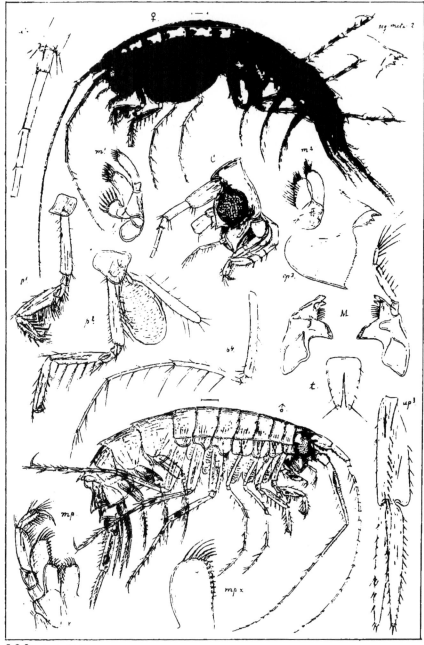

G.O.Sars autogr. Melphidippella macera, (Norman)

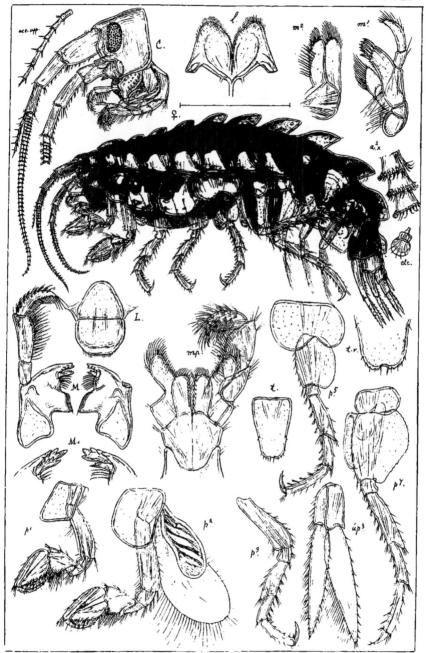

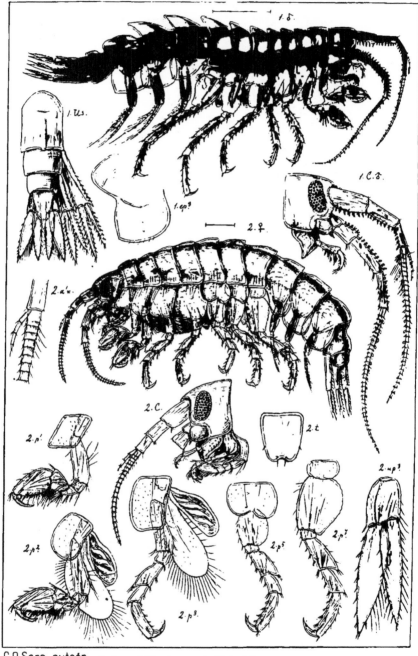

G.O Sars autogr.

1. Amathilla homari, (Fabr.) ♂.
2. Amathilla angulosa, (Rathke.)

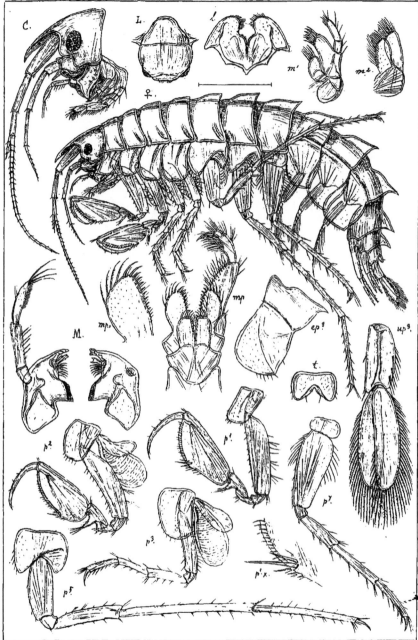

Gammaracanthus relictus, G.O.Sars.

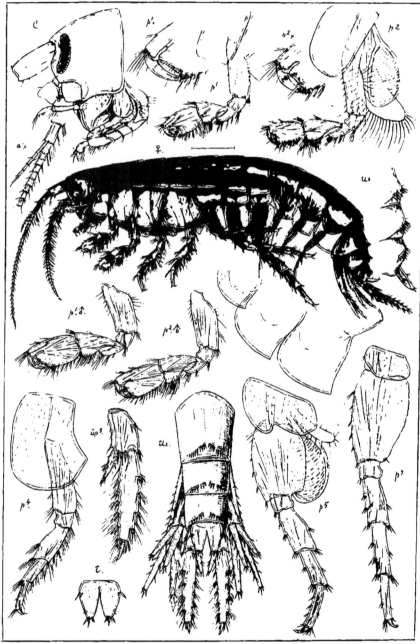

Gammarus marinus, Leach.

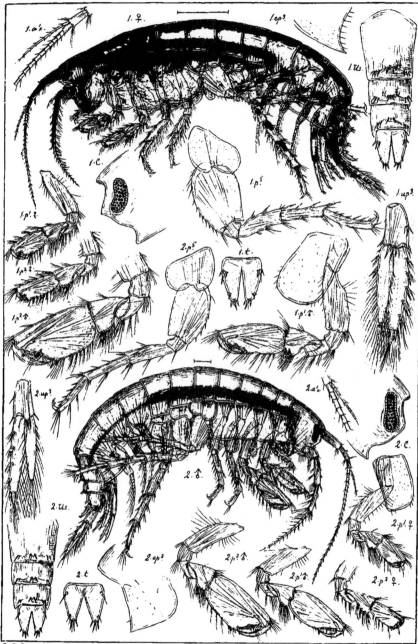

1. Gammarus locusta, (Lin.)
2. Gammarus campylops, Leach.

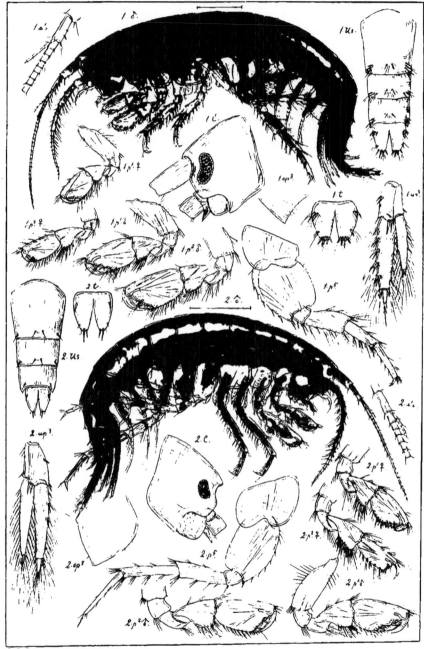

G.O.Sars autogr.
1. Gammarus Duebeni, Lilljeb.
2. Gammarus pulex, (Lin.)

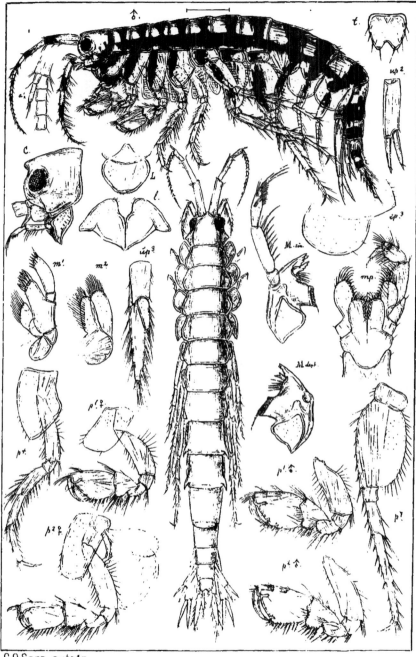

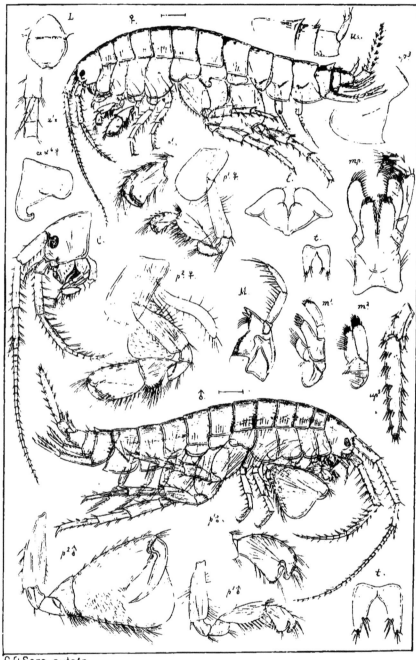

G.O.Sars autogr.　　Melita palmata, (Mont.)

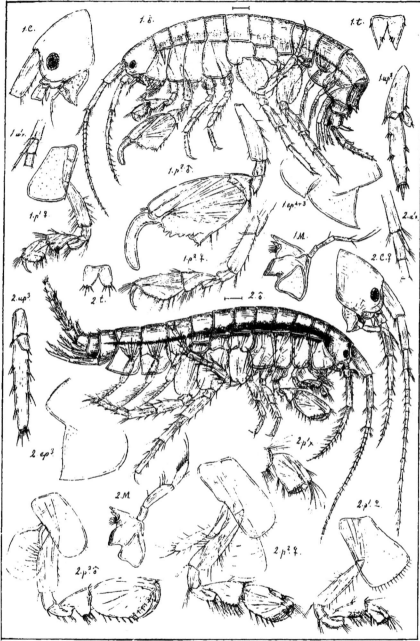

G.O.Sars autogr.

1. Melita obtusata, (Mont.)
2. Melita pellucida, G.O.Sars.

G. O. Sars autogr

1. Melita dentata. (Kröyer).
2. Eriopisa elongata. (Bruzel.)

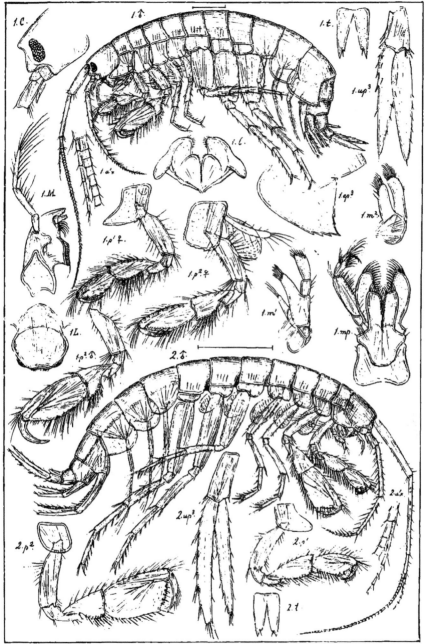

G.O.Sars autogr.   1. Maera Othonis, (M-Edw.)
                   2. Maera Lovéni, (Bruzel.)

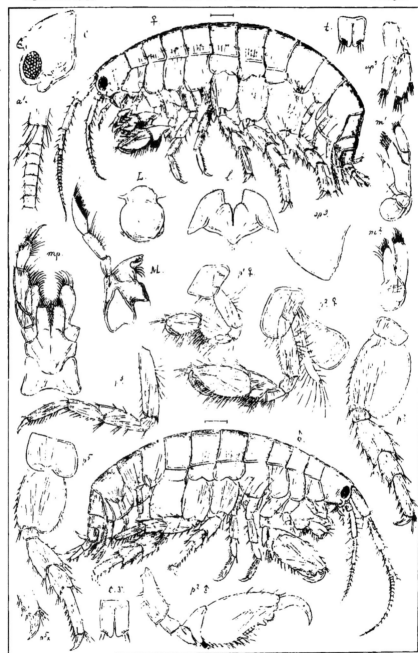

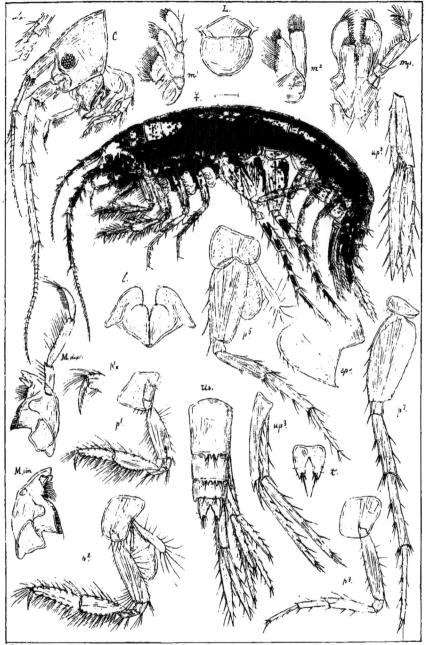

Cheirocratus Sundewalli, (Rathke.)

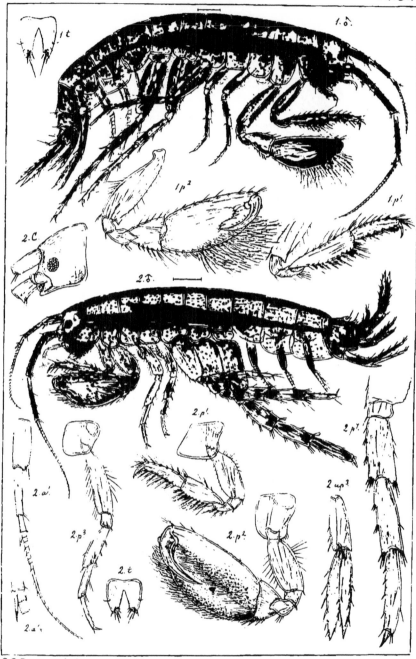

G.O.Sars autogr.　1. Cheirocratus Sundewalli, (Rathke)♂.
2. Cheirocratus robustus, n.sp.

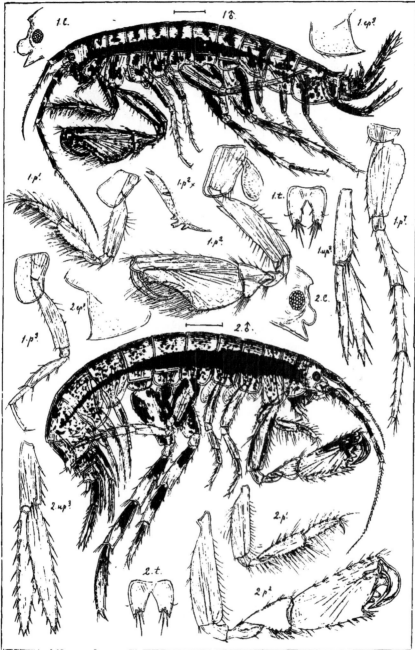

1. Cheirocratus intermedius, n.sp.
2. Cheirocratus assimilis, (Lilljeb).

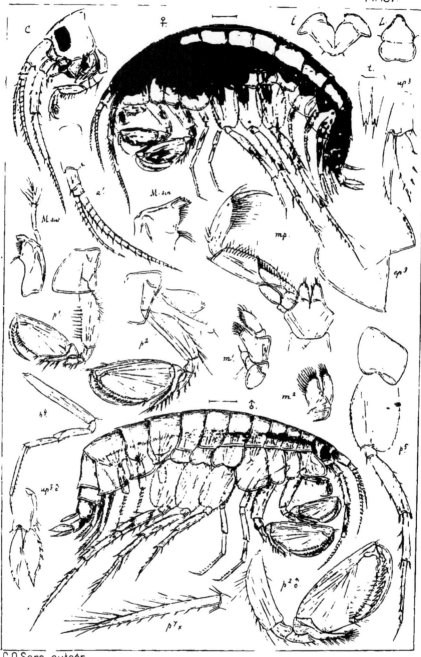

Liljeborgia pallida, Sp. Bate.

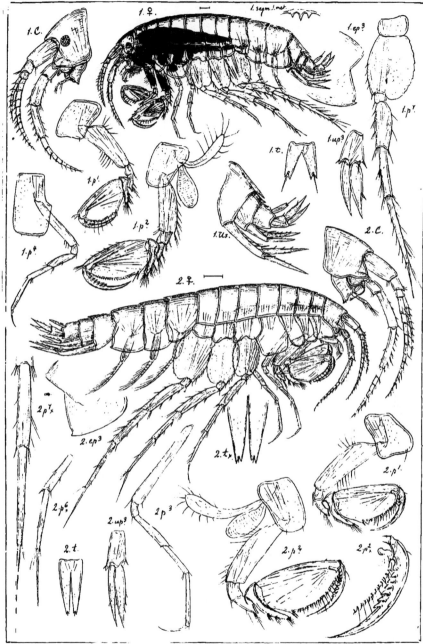

GO Sars autogr.
1. Lilljeborgia Kinahani, (Sp. Bate).
2. Lilljeborgia macronyx, n.sp.

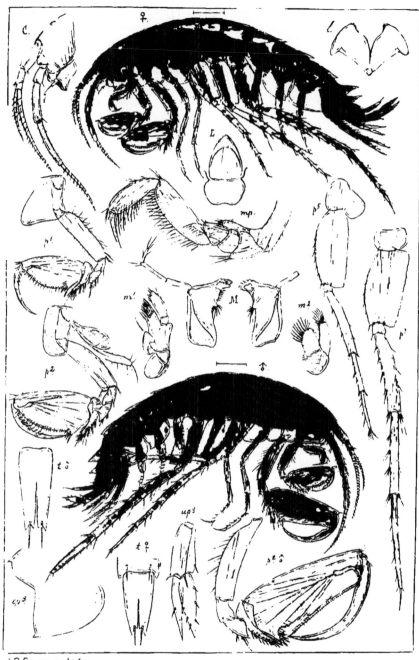

Liljeborgia fissicornis, (M.Sars).

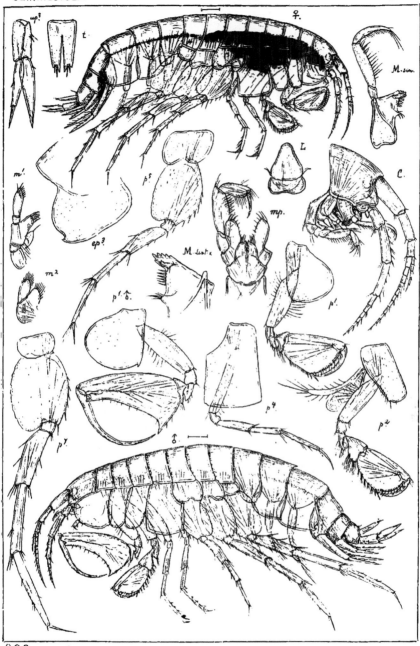

G.O.Sars autogr. Idunella æqvicornis, G.O.Sars.

G.O.Sars autogr.   Microdeutopus anomalus, (Rathke).

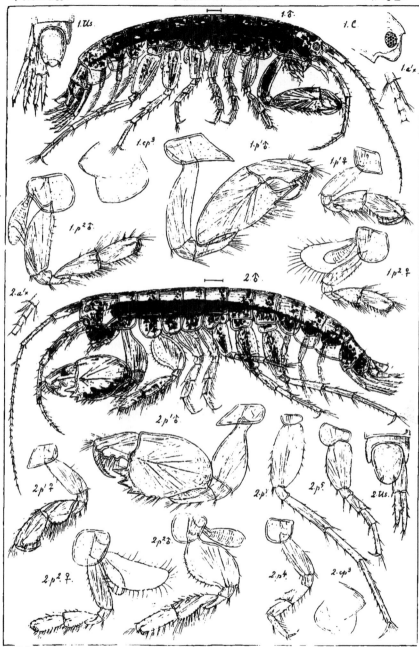

G O Sars autogr.

1 Microdeutopus propinqvus, n. sp.
2. Microdeutopus gryllotalpa, Costa

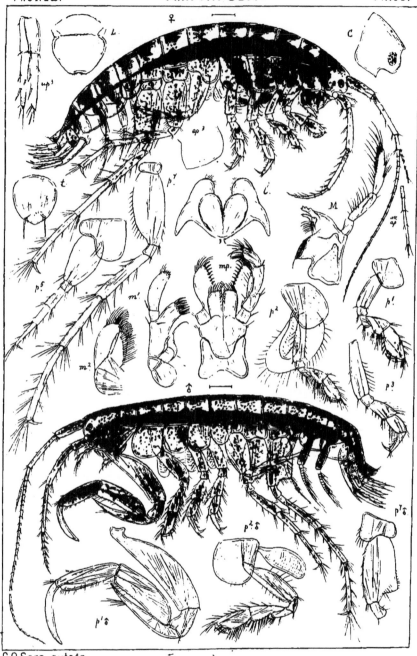

Aora gracilis, Sp. Bate.

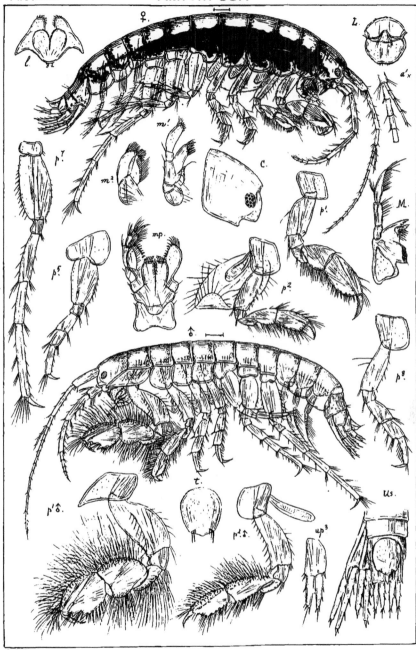

G.O.Sars autogr.

Autonoë Websterij (Sp. Bate).

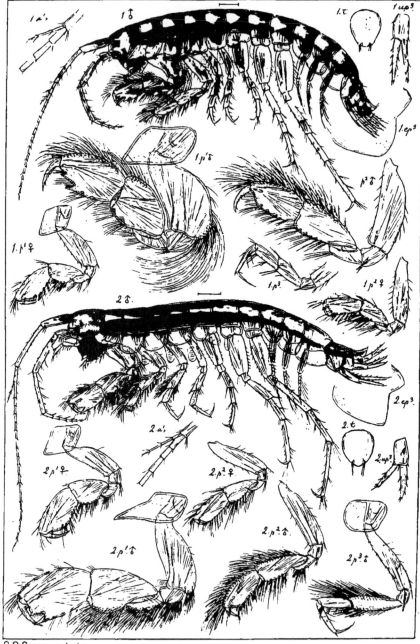

G.O.Sars autogr.

1. Autonoë longipes, (Lilljeborg).
2. Autonoë megacheir, (G.O.Sars.)

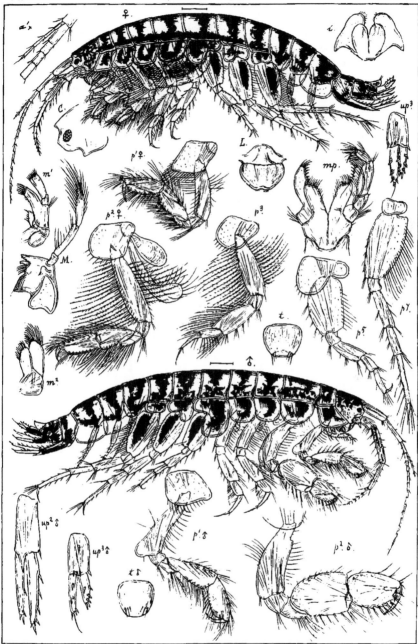

Protomedeia fasciata, Kröyer.

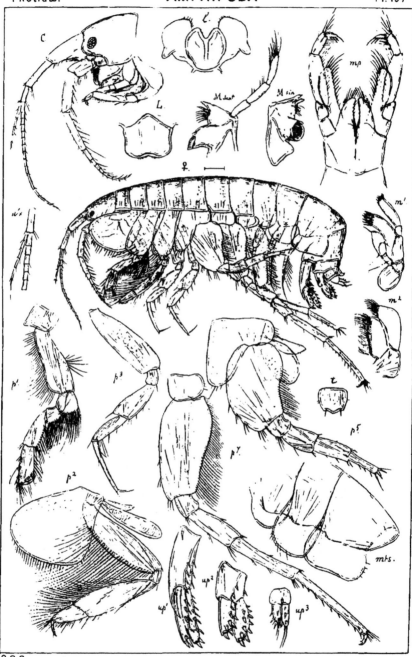

G.O.Sars autogr.

Leptocheirus pilosus, Zaddach.

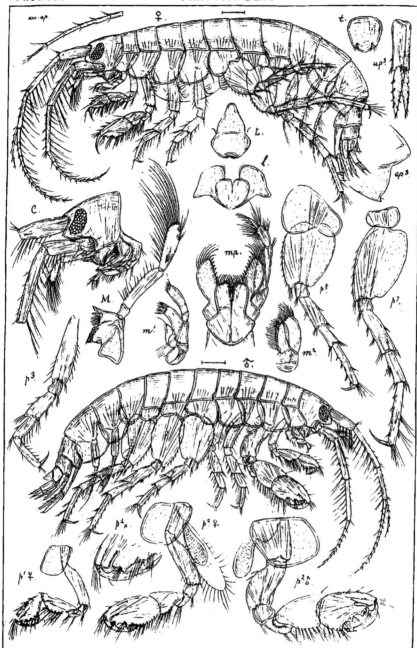

Gammaropsis erythrophthalma, (Lilljeborg).

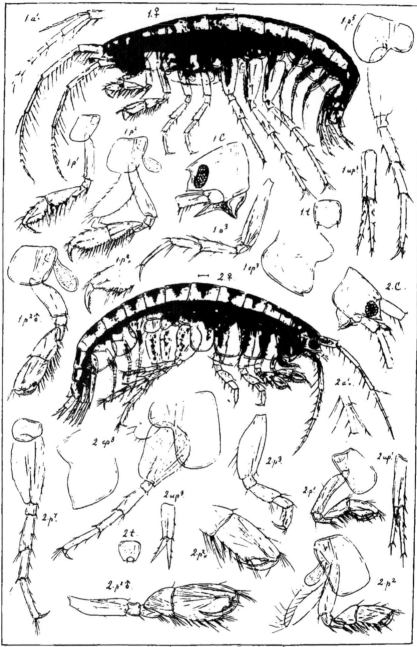

G.O.Sars autogr.

1. Gammaropsis melanops, G.O.Sars.

2. Gammaropsis nana, n.sp.

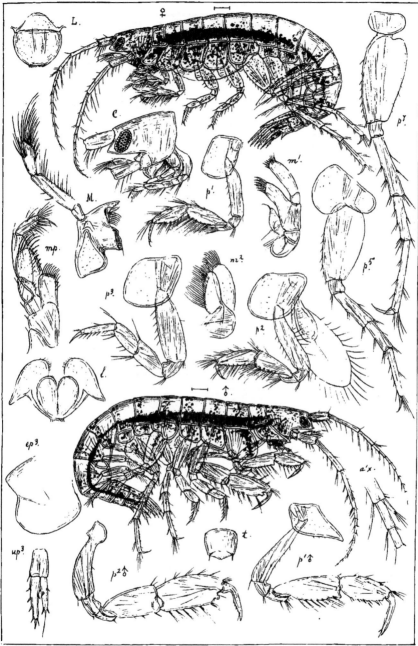

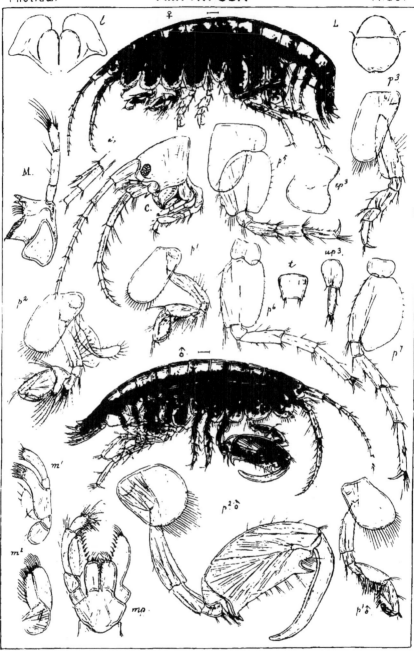

G O Sars autogr.   Microprotopus maculatus, Norman.

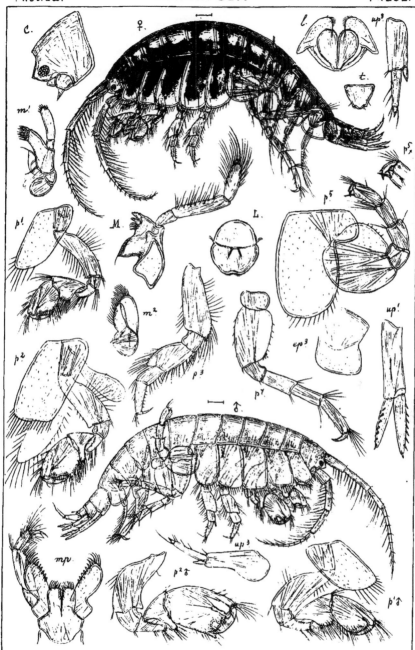

Photis Reinhardi, Kröyer.

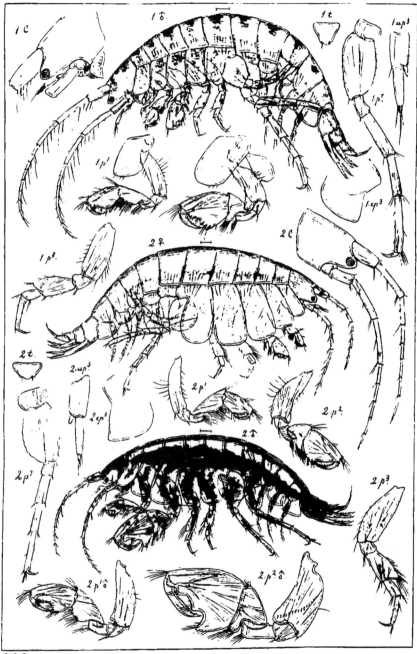

1. Photis longicaudata, (Sp. Bate).
2. Photis tenuicornis, G.O.Sars.

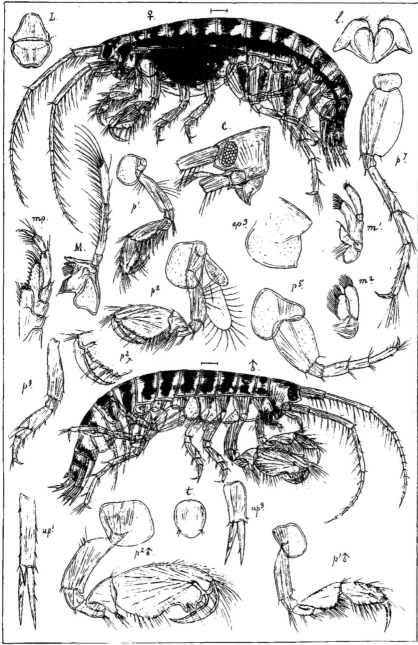

Podoceropsis Sophiæ, Boeck.

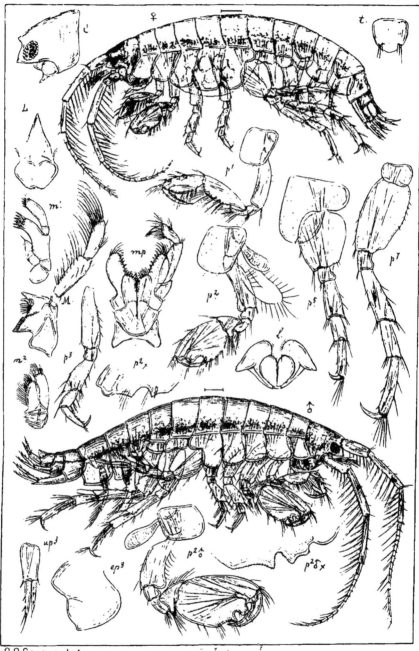

G.O.Sars autogr.   Podoceropsis excavata, (Sp.Bate).

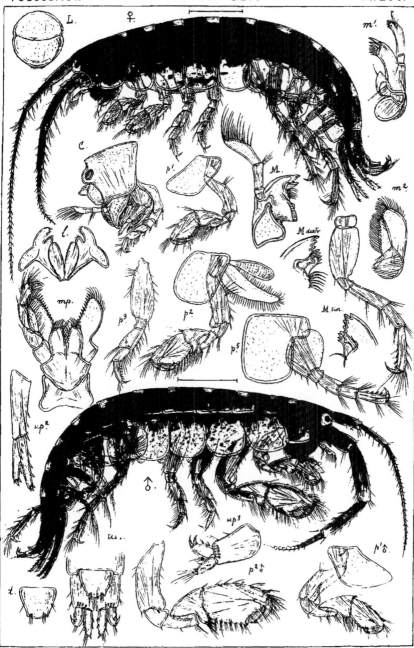

Amphithoë rubricata, (Mont.)

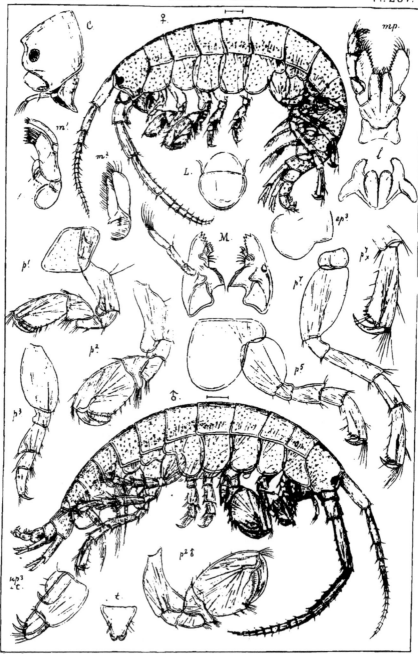

Pleonexes gammaroides, Sp. Bate.

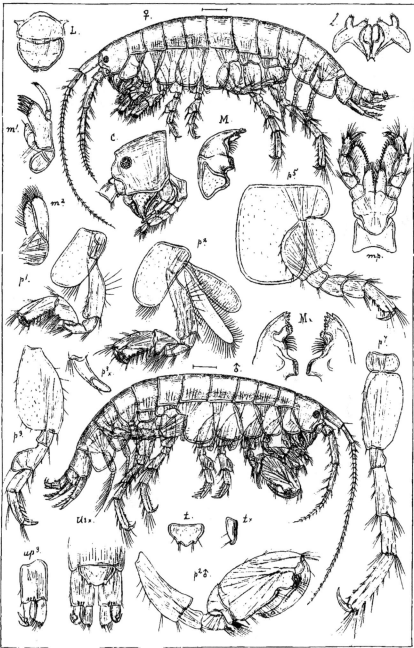

G O Sars autogr.

Sunamphithoë conformata, Sp. Bate.

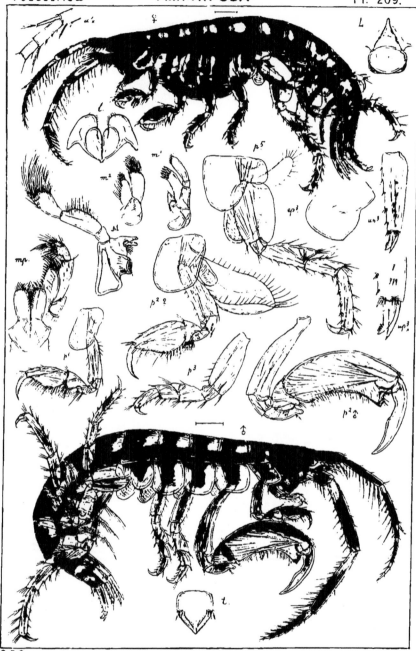

G O Sars autogr. Ischyrocerus angvipes, Kröyer.

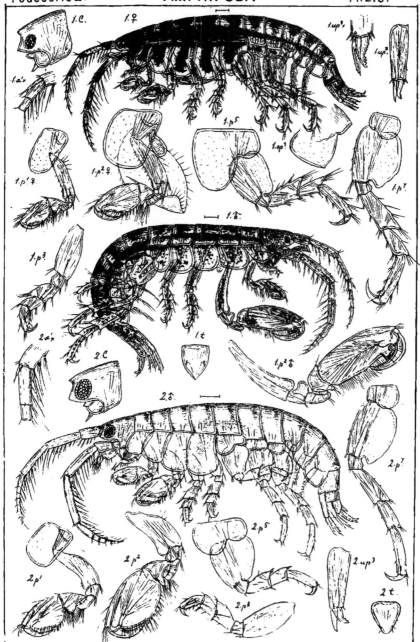

1. Ischyrocerus minutus, Lilljeborg.
2. Ischyrocerus megalops, n.sp.

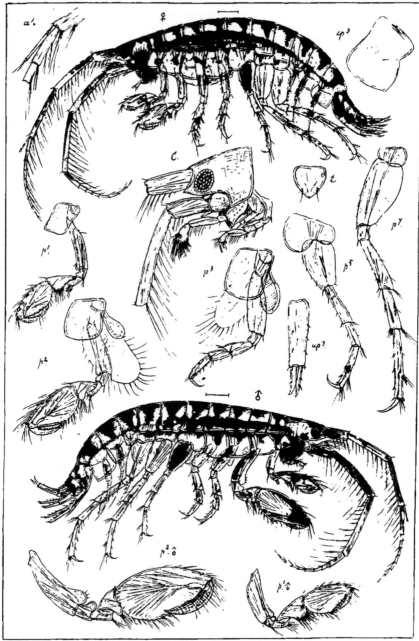

Ischyrocerus megacheir, (Boeck).

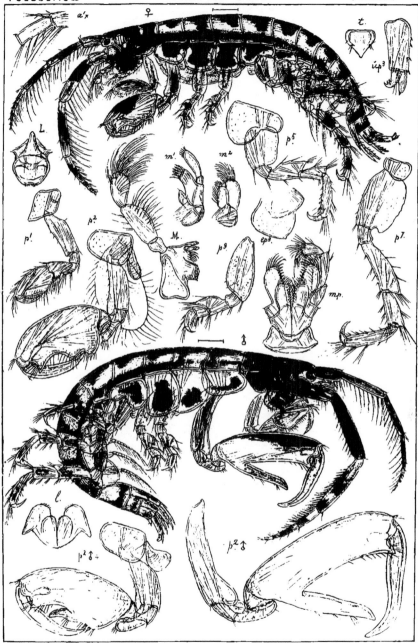

G.O.Sars autogr.   Podocerus falcatus, (Mont.)

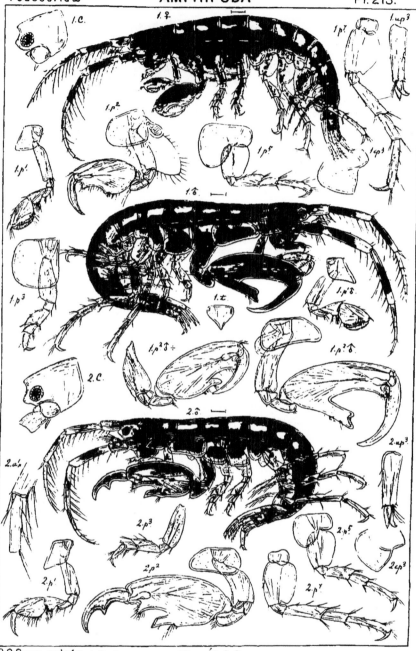

1. Podocerus pusillus, G.O.Sars.
2. Podocerus odontonyx, n. sp.

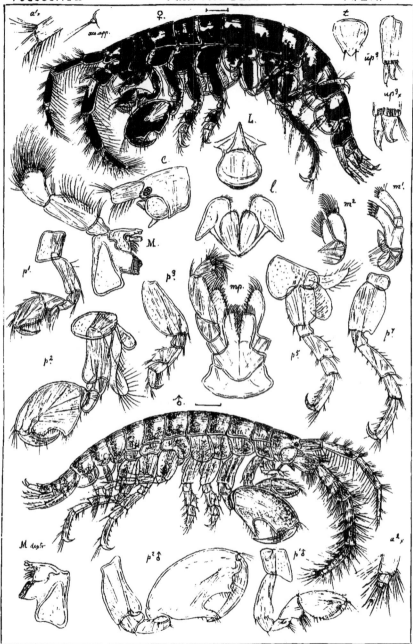

G.O.Sars autogr.   Janassa capillata, (Rathke).

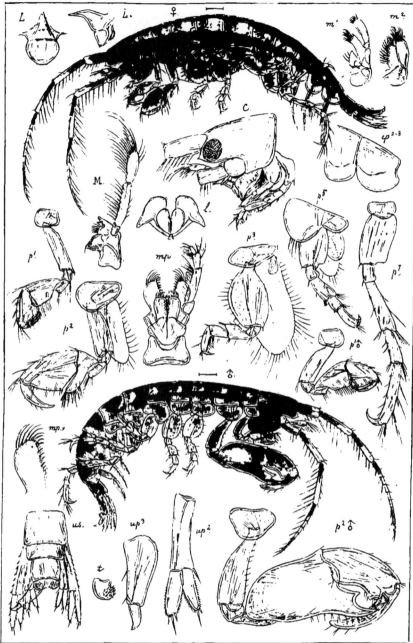

GO Sars autogr.   Erichthonius abditus, (Templet.)

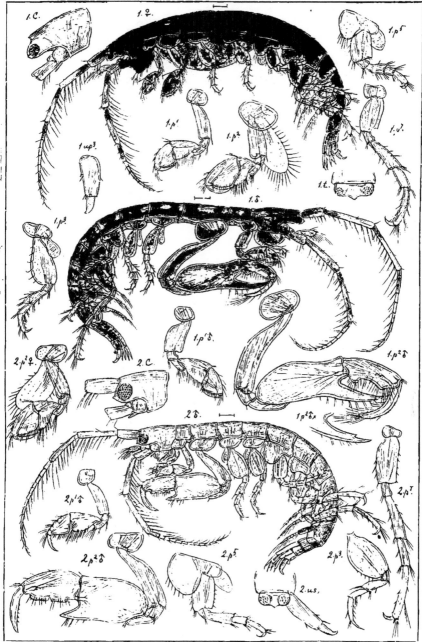

G.O.Sars autogr. 1. Erichthonius difformis, M-Edw.
2. Erichthonius Hunteri, Sp. Bate.

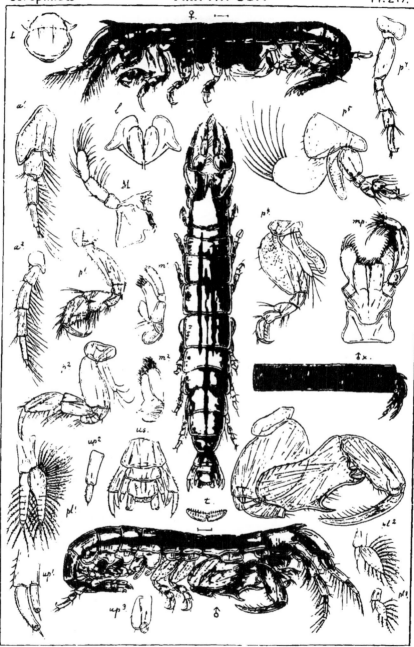

G O Sars autogr   Cerapus crassicornis (Sp Bate.)

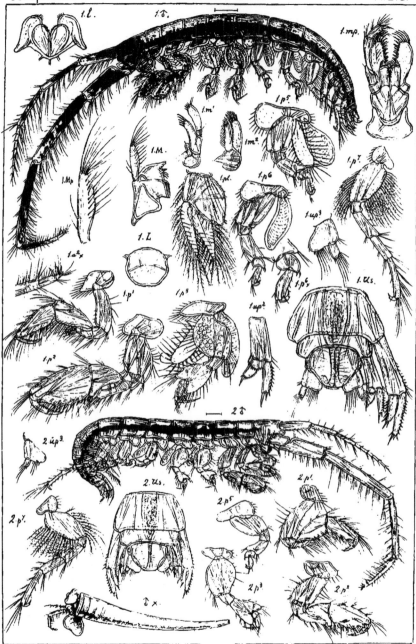

1. Siphonoecetes Colletti, Boeck.
2. Siphonoecetes pallidus, G.O.Sars.

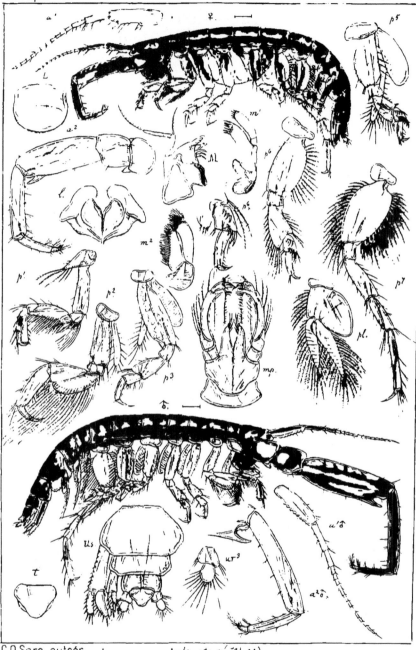

G.O.Sars autogr.

Corophium grossipes (Linné).

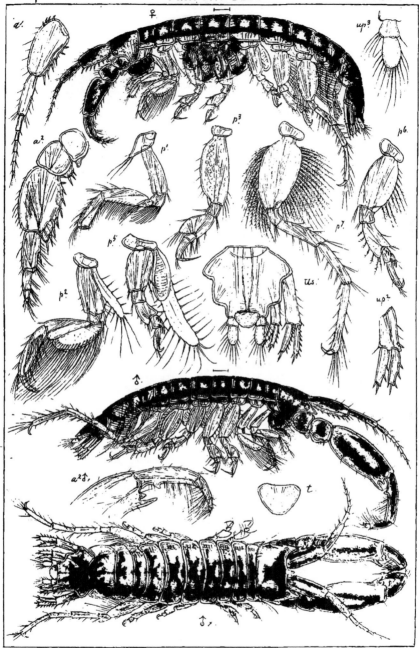

G.O.Sars autogr.   Corophium crassicorne, Bruzel.

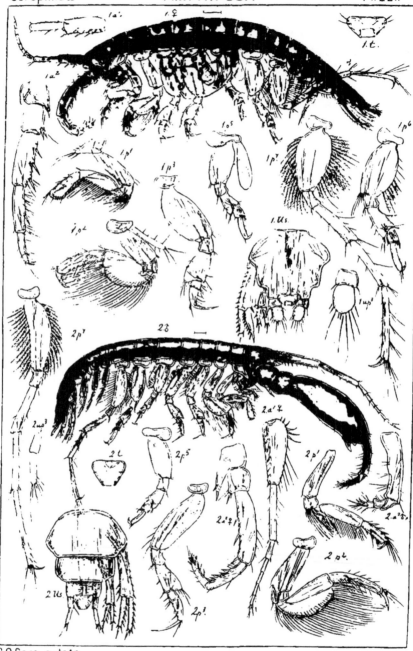

G.O.Sars autogr.

1. Corophium Bonelli, M.-Edw.
2. Corophium affine, Bruzel.

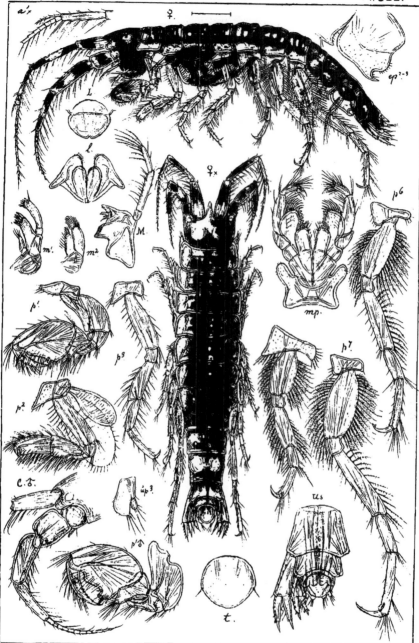

Unciola leucopis, (Kröyer.)

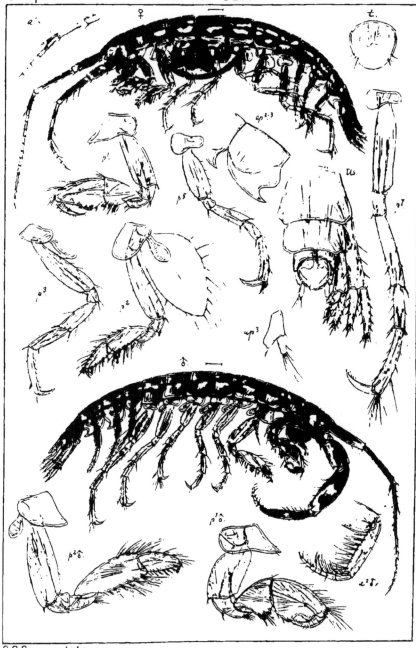

G O Sars autogr.   Unciola planipes, Norm.

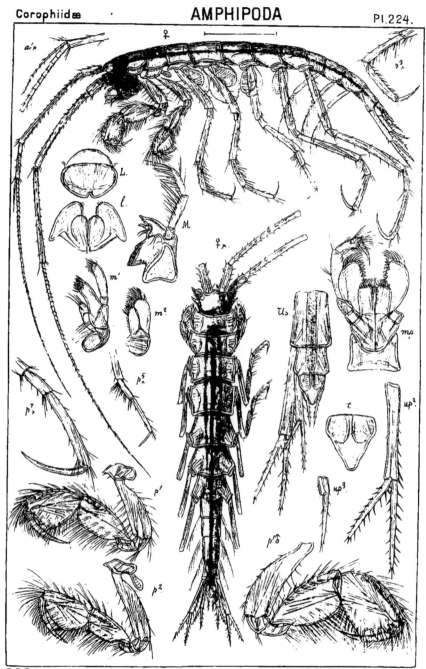

Neohela monstrosa, (Boeck).

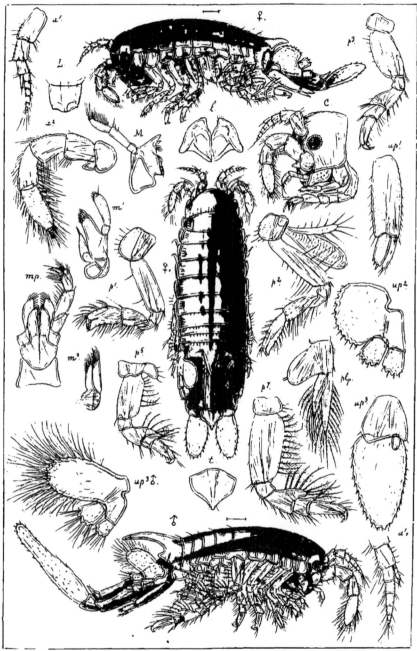

G.O. Sars autogr.　　Chelura terebrans, Phil.

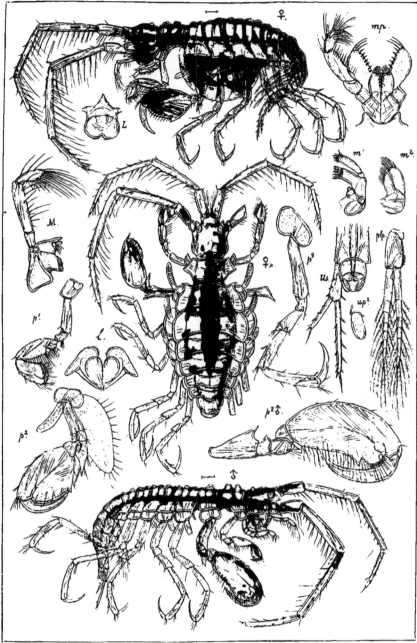

G.O.Sars autogr.

Lætmatophilus tuberculatus, Bruz.

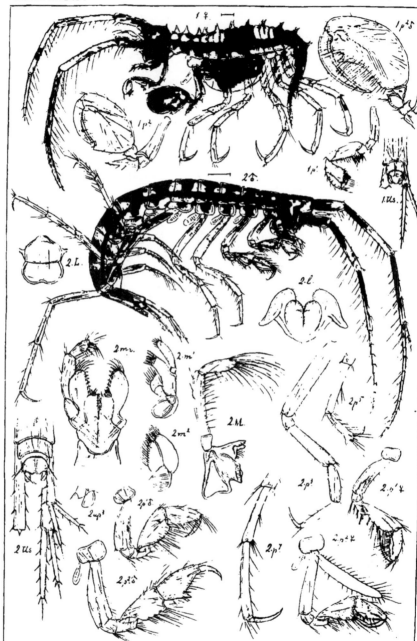

1. Lætmatophilus armatus. (Norm.).
2. Xenodice Frauenfeldti, Boeck.

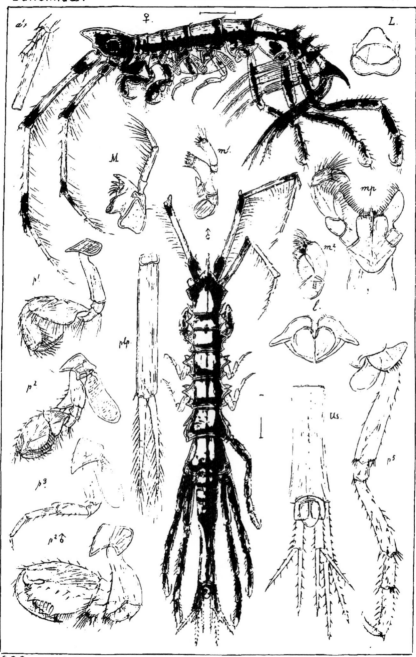

Dulichia spinosissima, Kröyer.

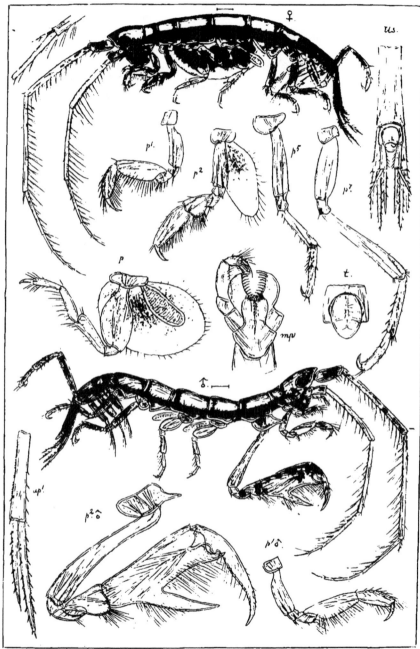

G.O.Sars autogr. Dulichia porrecta, Sp. Bate.

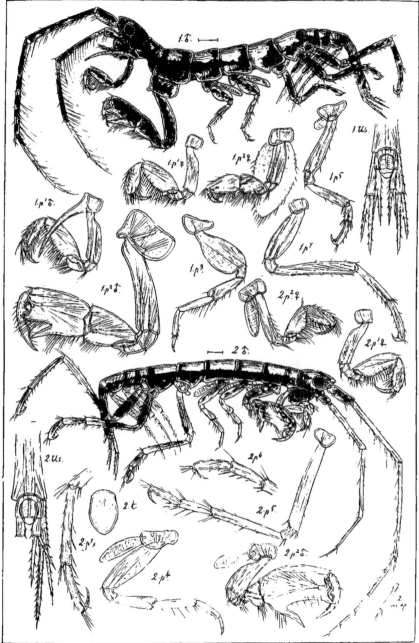

1. Dulichia monacantha, Metzger.
2. Dulichia curticauda, Boeck.

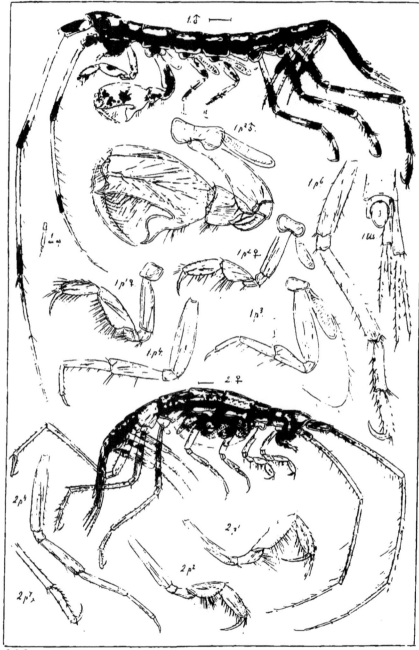

GO Sars autogr   1. Dulichia falcata, Sp. Bate.
2. Dulichia nordlandica, Boeck. ♀.

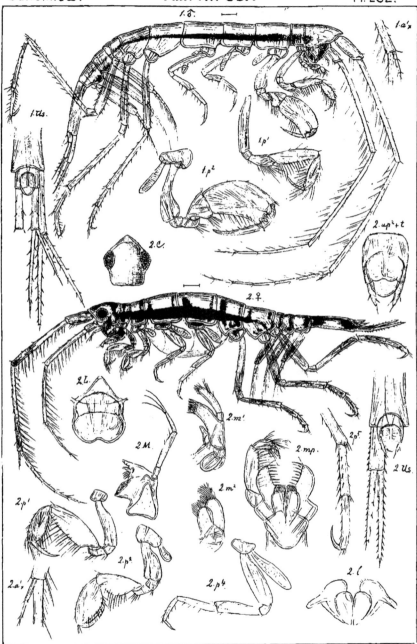

1. Dulichia nordlandica, Boeck ♂
2. Paradulichia typica, Boeck.

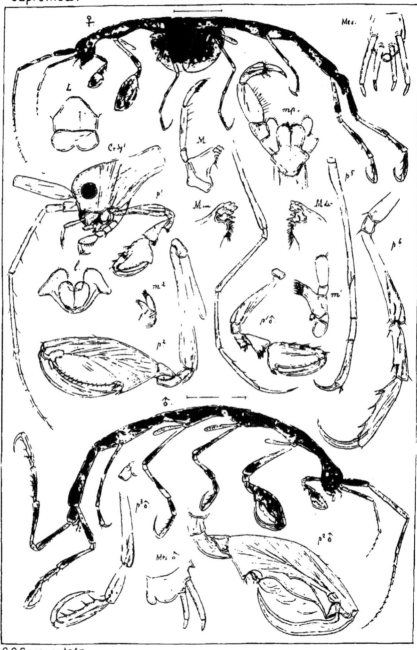

G O Sars autogr.   Proto pedata, (Müll.)

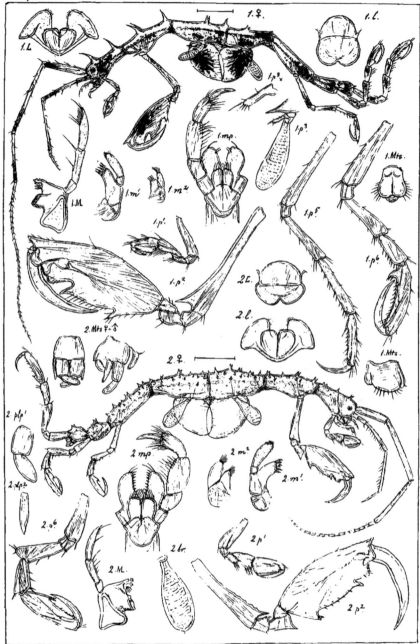

G.O.Sars autogr.

1. Protella phasma, (Mont.)
2. Ægina echinata, Boeck.

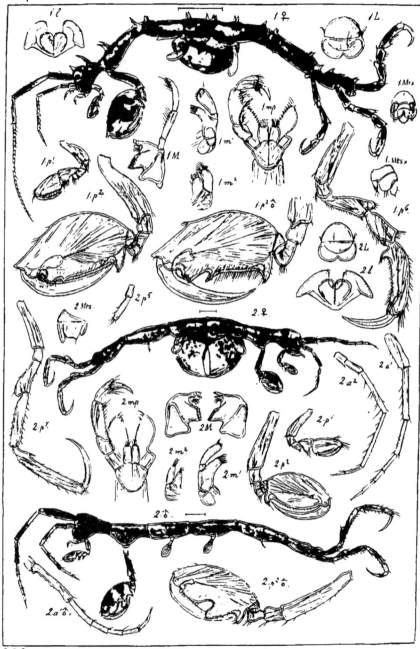

1. Æginella spinosa, Boeck.
2. Podalirius typicus, Kröyer.

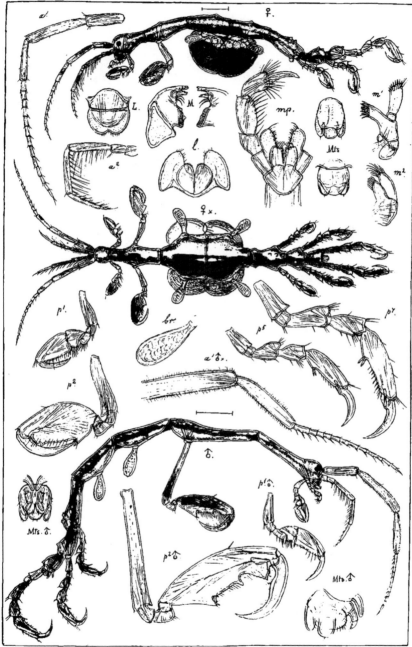

Caprella linearis, (Lin.)

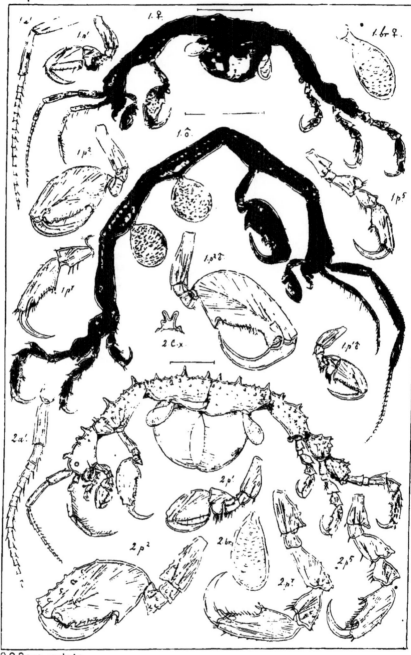

1. Caprella septentrionalis, Kröyer.
2. Caprella punctata, Boeck.

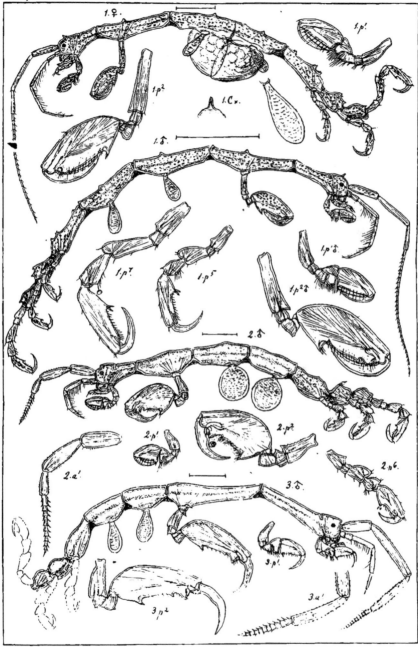

1. Caprella monocera, n. sp.
2. Caprella Lovéni, Boeck.
3. Caprella æqvilibra, Say.

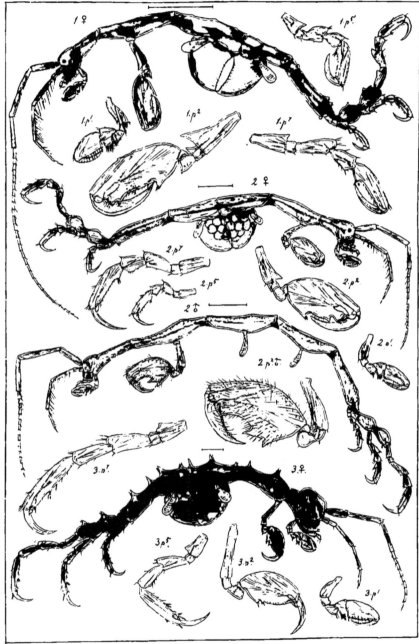

G.O.Sars autogr 1. Caprella microtuberculata, G.O.Sars.
                 2. Caprella ciliata, G.O.Sars.
                 3. Caprella acanthifera, Leach.

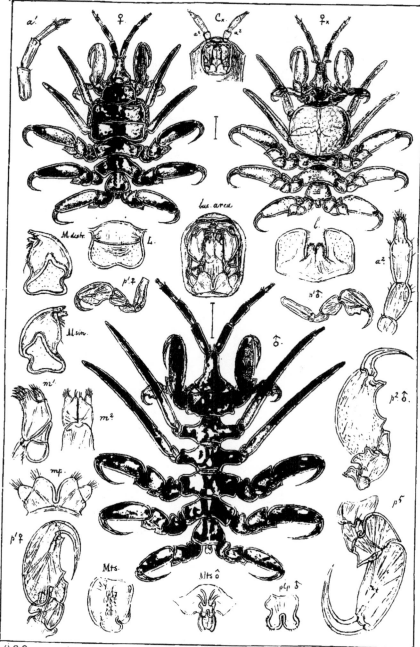

G.O.Sars autogr.

Cyamus boopis, Lütken.

G.O.Sars autogr.

1. Normanion amblyops. n. sp.
2. Aristias microps, n. sp.

1. Aristias megalops, n, sp.
2 Perrierella audouiniana, (Sp.Bate.)

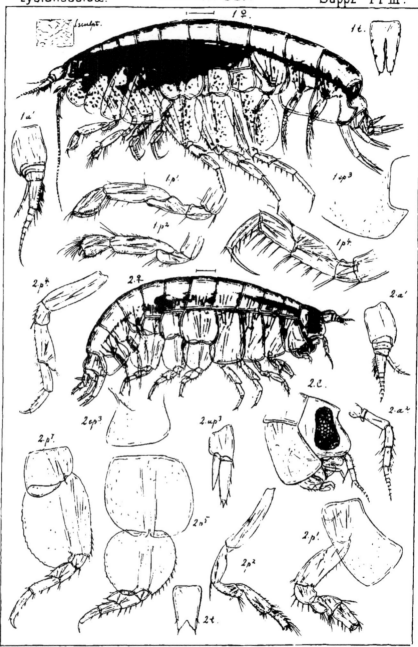

1. Hippomedon robustus, n. sp.
2. Orchomene Hanseni, Meinert.

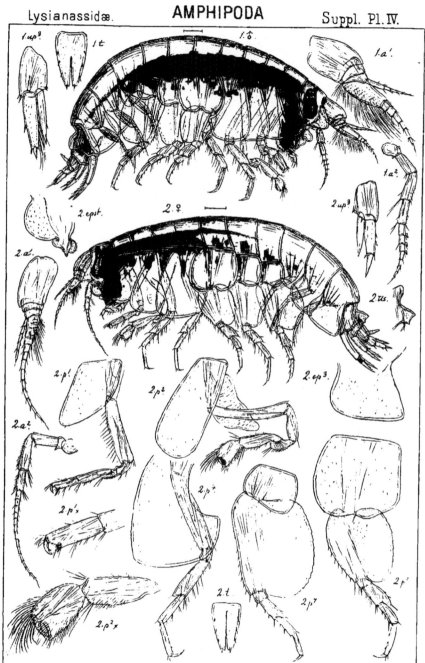

1. Orchomene serratus, Boeck. ♂
2. Tryphosa compressa, G. O Sars.

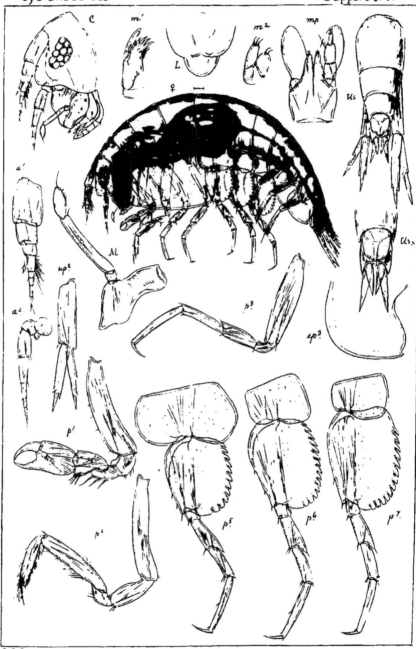

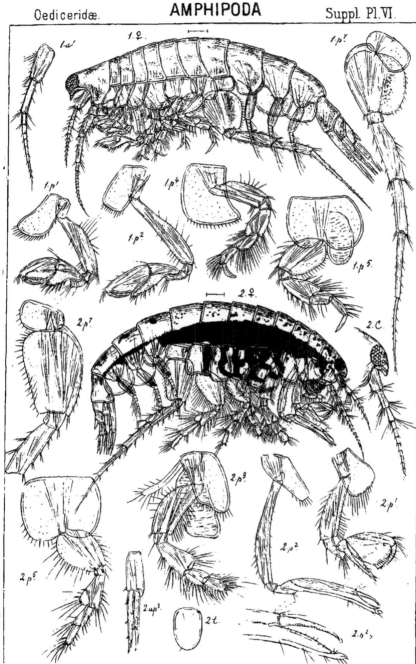

G.O.Sars autogr.

1 Monoculodes Schneideri, n.sp.
2. Pontocrates arenarius, (Sp Bate) ♀

1. Pontocrates arenarius,(Sp.Bate) ♂.
2. Pontocrates altamarinus,(Sp.Bate.)

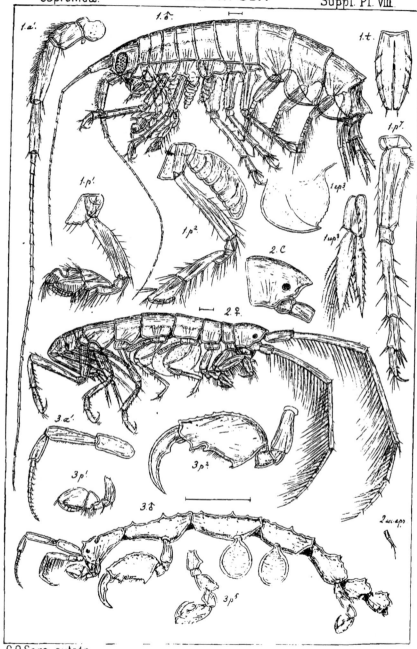

1. Tritæta gibbosa, (Sp.Bate) ♂.
2. Dulichia Normani, n. sp.
3. Caprella punctata, Boeck ♂.

Prospectus.

The undersigned, who for many years has been especially engaged in the study of the various groups of Crustacea, and who, on his many journeys of research, has been enabled to make himself especially familiar with the species represented in the northern fauna, hereby begs to invite Norwegian and foreign zoologists to subscribe to a complete work on the Crustacea of Norway. In this work, the author will characterise, as concisely as possible, all the Norwegian species hitherto known and, what is of great importance, the descriptions will be accompanied by carefully drawn figures of all the forms. The lack of good plates has hitherto made the study of this interesting class of animals very difficult, and, in many cases, has caused sad confusion in the synonymy. It is now the author's intention to try to make the species belonging to the fauna of Norway easily recognisable and definable, which, much better than by the most elaborate descriptions, may undoubtedly be brought about by habitus figures, true to nature, and of sufficient size and clearness. All the plates will be prepared by the author himself, by the autographic method applied by him very successfully during a series of years, and, as by this means the expense of lithographing will be avoided, the work can be delivered, richly illustrated, at a comparatively low price. As the state of affairs at our University, for the time, is not such as to allow one to suppose that a work of this extent can be expected to be published by the University within a reasonable time, the author is obliged to adopt the mode of publication suggested here, and does not doubt but that the undertaking will meet with a favourable reception by foreign zoologists, and that no difficulties will arise to prevent its being completed at a comparatively early date. To obtain as large a distribution as possible it will be written entirely in the English language. — As stated, the letterpress descriptions will be as concise as possible, and will be chiefly confined to short diagnoses of the families, genera and species, critical remarks as to the synonyms, and information as to occurrence and distribution of the species. The utmost

... will be reserved in preparing ... plates ... as the ... ... offering
the author ... to ... to the many special features published by ...,
... the government method has been used.

The ... plates will now prove the order ... to which ...
... or all, in time ... which the determination of ... ...
with the greatest difficulties and which therefore require a thorough ...
The numbers will appear at as short intervals as possible. As all
plates are prepared ... and the ... are thus quite independent
... the explanation or ... of the ... All ... will be ... used to
best advantage. The habitus ... plates, which in ... ...
living specimens, will thus ... fully drawn, showing the ... of ... ...
... characteristic for each species, not as is usually the case only ...
... ... and there will ... be given, on a greatly enlarged scale, detail ...
of the ... characteristic parts. The author ... especially thinks it ...
the greatest importance to give correct representations of the ...
... of the oral part in the ... ... the classification
... Amphipoda ... ... to be based upon this character. In a ...
number of copies, the plates will be coloured from the original ...
by the author.

G. O. Sars,

Professor at the University of Christiania, Norway.

The above mentioned work will be published by the undersigned ...
... price for every number of plates with corresponding ... to ... ...
letterpress description, in ... ... will for ... ...
pp. 25 ... postage to one pr. number. The subscription ... ...
vol. I Amphipoda ...

This volume will contain about 40 numbers, and it will ...
be completed in the course of one or two years. A few copies ...
... plates ... be obtained but the price of each will ...
materially greater.

The work can be ordered through any bookseller or direct ... ...
publisher.

Christiania, June 1890.

Alb. Cammermeyer,

Carl Johansgade 41.